Food
Of The
Spirit

*World Travel and the Everday Miracles
of Personal Transformation*

STEPHANIE WEEKS

BALBOA.
PRESS
A DIVISION OF HAY HOUSE

ISV: Scripture taken from the Holy Bible: International Standard Version®. Copyright © 1996-forever by The ISV Foundation. ALL RIGHTS RESERVED INTERNATIONALLY. Used by permission.

NIV: Scripture quotations marked (NIV) are taken from the Holy Bible, New International Version®, NIV®. Copyright © 1973, 1978, 1984, 2011 by Biblica, Inc.™ Used by permission of Zondervan. All rights reserved worldwide. www. zondervan.com The "NIV" and "New International Version" are trademarks registered in the United States Patent and Trademark Office by Biblica, Inc.

ESV: Scripture quotations are from the ESV® Bible (The Holy Bible, English Standard Version®), copyright © 2001 by Crossway, a publishing ministry of Good News Publishers. Used by permission. All rights reserved.

NKJV: Scripture taken from the New King James Version®. Copyright © 1982 by Thomas Nelson. Used by permission. All rights reserved.

Balboa Press books may be ordered through booksellers or by contacting:

Balboa Press
A Division of Hay House
1663 Liberty Drive
Bloomington, IN 47403
www.balboapress.com
1 (877) 407-4847

Print information available on the last page.

ISBN: 978-1-5043-9484-0 (sc)
ISBN: 978-1-5043-9485-7 (hc)
ISBN: 978-1-5043-9511-3 (e)

Library of Congress Control Number: 2017919658

Balboa Press rev. date: 04/04/2018

Why this book?

We all have valuable lessons to learn in life. Mine may be completely different from yours. Some may be the same. No matter what circumstances you or I might be facing, currently or in the future, key principles can be applied to ensure our ability not only to embrace but also benefit from whatever our situation may bring. Three brief sentences summarize those principles: 1) Surrendering fear, gives more space to love; 2) Receiving forgiveness is woven together with our ability to offer forgiveness to others; and 3) Recognizing that God has perfectly designed us to be His light to the world enables Him to work in and through us more easily and miraculously.

You have the ability not only to embrace these fundamental principles but also to share them— and God's love—with others.

It's an amazing calling to live life full out. Will you accept it? What if I told you that God would be guiding you every step of the way?

Personal development and spiritual growth can often seem not just burdensome and difficult but even overwhelming or impossible. It doesn't need to be. There is a clear and manageable path to achieve the inner growth that takes much of the stress and fear out of the equation.

We all know the old saying, "Hindsight is 20/20." But what does that actually mean? Have you ever noted, after the fact, that you'd ignored obvious cues that should have tipped you off concerning a mistake you made or a wrong path you took? Who hasn't? But when we learn to lean on God and let him walk before us, we stop having to concern ourselves as much with being on the right path. Instead, we start to trust God simply to guide us to where we need to be.

In *Food Of The Spirit*, I will share a great deal of my real-life experiences with you. For the last decade, I've been fortunate enough to travel the world, experiencing all that makes this life a wonderful soul experience. I'm ready to transport you to exotic places around the globe that represent chapters of spiritual healing in my own life and in the lives of those around me. My hope is that as you read my stories of personal growth, you'll get a powerful glimpse into how to embrace your own.

Everyone faces crises in life that will test their faith in themselves, the world, and their Creator. Those crossroads are where we each have the ability to learn the most. Yet, because such experiences tend to involve discomfort or even pain, we often run from them and miss important opportunities to grow. Our spirit's journey through this life is meant to engage in an array of invaluable lessons that ultimately enhance and fulfill our experience. Will we run from what is offered to us and miss out? Or will we welcome and benefit from the opportunities we're given?

The world is a big place. It may even feel like a scary place. Actually, though, the world is very small, and it has the potential to be highly welcoming and supportive, since everyone in it has the same fundamental desires and needs. Unfortunately, we often overlook this truth when we allow our fear and pain to overwhelm us. Consequently, we also miss the crucial fact that this moment is all we have; we are not promised tomorrow or next year. But as you'll discover as we traverse the pages of this book together, that's o.k. It turns out that being in the present moment is all that our spirit actually needs.

A Beginner's Mind Is Limitless

I place no limits and no restrictions on all that I intend
to accomplish and become from here on in.

— Dr. Wayne W. Dyer

Beginners come to learn. And as beginners, we come to the plate
with a fresh view point and openness. So much can happen in one
day. We are born in one day. We die in one day. We can change
the trajectory of our lives and our outlook in one day. *Anything* can
happen in just one day.

You are a miracle. Your life is a miracle, and everything around you
lends way to more miracles, if you are willing to do just one thing:
acknowledge things as they are.

On the path of discovering miracles, it is wise to see the miracles
that already occur around us each and every day. As we witness and
adopt a grateful heart toward these daily miracles, an amazing thing
starts to happen. Our perspective is opened—and we are blessed
with—more miracles.

For example, remember the miracle of each new day. When you
woke up today, life was full of endless possibilities. It is full of those
same possibilities—and more—as you read these words. But if you
do not see or grasp those possibilities, if you do nothing with them,

they will only ever be possibilities. The first step is to greet each day with gratitude, remembering that it is a new opportunity to grow, discover, and love abundantly.

In achieving this shift, you will likely experience things outside of your comfort zone. There's another one of those scary prospects. But before you decide it's just too hard and put this book down, know that it's easier than you think, and that embracing this same perspective shift will allow you to do all kinds of things you never imagined possible, creating something that will literally live on forever. Nourishing the soul with the food of the spirit goes beyond what we see in the here and now. It reaches to the depths of Creation, changing the way life is experienced for everyone moving forward. Creating a positive impact on the world never dies.

Before you read another word, I have a question for you.

Are you wasting time, trying to solve problems that don't exist?

Everyday Miracles

The authentic self is the soul made visible.

— Sarah Ban Breathnach

It is spiritually vital to conduct ourselves from a place of true authenticity. It is possible to make choices that help us to become more of who we are—who we were meant to be. Eminent psychologist Carl Rogers referred to this process as self-actualization. A similar process is found in many of the great spiritual traditions, many of which teach that we were created with a purpose and are meant to spend our entire life realizing and fulfilling it. Achieving that end requires nourishing our spirit with the right kinds of food for the soul. The result is healing and a deeper connection with our Creator.

A famous passage from Christian scripture, Galatians 5:22-23, says: "The fruit of the Spirit is *love, joy, peace, patience, kindness, goodness, faithfulness, gentleness, and self-control. There is no law against these things! (International Standard Version)*

This passage is a remarkable description of the abundance that is available to us if we will only open ourselves to what can be accomplished in and through us. In this state of being we flourish, we are not concerned with what has been or what will be; we are simply as God intended, remaining, or abiding, in this moment, and trusting that the right things will happen.

But what are we really talking about when we use the word *abundance?*

Most people define abundance as an accumulation of tangible items; *stuff*—and a lot of it. There's nothing wrong with having stuff—if it facilitates the expansive liberation of our soul. Yet, in many cases, stuff creates merely illusionary abundance.

True abundance in our lives is spiritual. Have you ever noticed that spiritually abundant people are at peace with who they are and where they are in their life journey? It's because living in a state of abundance reframes one's perspective on external circumstances; whether good or bad, those circumstances do not subtract from the internal state of abundance. True abundance, therefore, is a state of being. It is a gift from our Creator and is not contingent on outside forces. Its essence cannot be diminished. No one can rob us of our abundance. Nor can they bestow more abundance upon us. There is more than enough to go around. In fact, there is an abundance of abundance. Everyone can live in abundance.

However, in order to accept and access abundance in our lives, there's something we do need to give up: the mentality of lack.

How do we do that?

It's easy and very human to get wrapped up in the world. It distracts us and frequently causes us to overlook what is right in front of us. That often leads to us feeling like we're without things we need or want—love, acceptance, opportunity, and any number of other vital things. When we adopt an attitude of abundance, we acknowledge issues when they arise. However, we choose not to get caught up in them. We refuse to identify with or be defined by issues or circumstances. Instead, we simply see them as they are and move beyond them.

How? By pausing consciously to remember what we want in life. If you want abundance, focus on the abundant areas in your life and circumstances. Negatively focusing on your problems will yield— you guessed it—more problems. Whatever you have your mind set to, you will discover that 'like attracts like'.

While there are many reasons for the learning opportunities we have in this life, a principal one is to reveal aspects of truth about ourselves *to* ourselves. When we enter this world we have a pre-determined amount of time, our lifetime, to learn the specific lessons that facilitate our growth and the healing of our soul. As we foster healing, we create space for more abundance to spring forth into our life. Essentially, we build a beneficial self-fulfilling prophecy. With each lesson learned, our way of thinking changes, sometimes in small ways, sometimes profoundly—allowing us to think and see life differently.

Remember: We're talking about a daily occurrence that derives from conscious choice, not something that happens once in a while if we're just lucky enough. One of our Creator's highest desires for us is enlightenment. Every moment gives us the opportunity to learn something new—about ourselves, about God, about the world. When we are aware of the transformation that is occurring we can always find something to be grateful for. When tough situations arise instead of feeling afraid or seeing ourselves as a victim, we can now ask "what is being revealed to me?" We are no longer waiting to arrive at a destination. Instead, we have planted our feet firmly on the path of learning and self-discovery. The journey *is* our destination.

In abundance we want for nothing. We want for nothing, because we carry within us the knowledge that we already have everything. The universe "has our back" and supplies what we need when we need it. Rather than feeling as though we're always missing something, in abundance we feel complete because we've adopted a spirit of gratitude and appreciation for what we already have and what we trust will be supplied. In knowing that we are of God we can want for nothing because we know that God's hand is in every circumstance, providing—even if that provision doesn't necessarily look as we might expect. Abundance enables us to impact our reality profoundly, with every word we utter.

Don't you long for unlimited freedom, joy, bliss—to experience heaven on Earth? It's all available. Not just a moment here and there, but a whole life's worth.

Action Steps:

Keep a gratitude journal. Each day give thanks for each blessing in your life. Take time each day to jot down the opportunities and possibilities before you.

Divine Appointments Can't Be Planned

We come this way but once.
We can either tiptoe through life and hope we get to death without being badly bruised or we can live a full, complete life achieving our goals and realizing our wildest dreams.

— Bob Proctor

Life is an interesting phenomenon. We go about each day as if we have unlimited time, thinking we can put things off until tomorrow and that *someday*—tomorrow, next week, next month, next year— we will accomplish all that we intend.

But take heed: No one is promised tomorrow. We are not even promised an hour from now. All we have is *this moment*, and what we *do* in this moment impacts all of the moments after it.

When I stopped several years ago to think about what I wanted to accomplish in the limited time I have in this life, I realized that my list was as long as a child's Christmas wish-list. The best way I could imagine to maximize the time I've been given was to travel. I wanted to be immersed in other cultures, their rituals, and to know the people with whom I share this life.

Today, what was once just a dream has become a marvelous reality. For a decade, now, I have been traveling the world experiencing all that makes this life a wonderful soul experience. I've had the pleasure of visiting 142 countries and counting. I've taken tango classes in Argentina, walked the Great Wall of China, gone scuba diving off the most exotic islands in the world, and fed kangaroos apples from my mouth in Australia. I've visited more temples, castles, and religious sites than I can count. Life has become a thrilling adventure! The strange, constant movement has become familiar.

Being a perpetual traveler was tough at first. Sure, it sounds like rainbows and butterflies flying around the world leading some sort of glamorous life. I don't want to discount the fun I've had. However, traveling isn't always what people think.

One key lesson I learned early on was that life could be very simple if I allowed it to be. For ten years, now, I have had in tow one carry on-sized bag with all the things I need. A major feat for any girl. I'm not bragging; I'm simply testifying to the fact that, as it turns out, material possessions are not what make life worth living. We live in a world where it's easy to get caught up in keeping up with the Joneses; who drives a fancier car, who has the biggest house, who has a seemingly perfect life. Yes, it is nice to have nice things. But in the end, none of that matters. My life is not normal by society's standards. However, I've put myself in a position to allow my immediate circumstances to be my greatest teacher.

"But…where is home?" you're likely asking. In one way, that's a hard question to answer. In another, it's utterly simple: Home is wherever I happen to be. Travel has forced me outside of my comfort zone, expanding my awareness, constantly demanding that I examine my beliefs and perspective in the realm of all possibility. Life happens with those in front of me, whoever they are, wherever I am.

I'm not saying travel is the path for everyone. The path you discover may not involve travel at all. In fact, it will likely be another kind of adventure entirely. We are all unique individuals, and your miraculous adventure will necessarily look different than mine. What I want to convey is simply that, again: This moment is all we have, we are not promised tomorrow or next year and that is okay because the present moment is enough.

The present moment, whatever it is, gives us the ability to choose happiness and love. It also gives us the opportunity to positively impact those with whom we come into contact. In fact, like no time ever before in history, we have the ability to reach people worldwide in an instant. That's a powerful reality! What you do with it won't just impact others, it will create your future. When I let go of controlling my life and began living in this flow, the world opened its magnificence to me. It will unquestionably do the same for you.

Life is a journey of discovery, and our everyday environment holds all the components of a sacred space of transformation. Every soul is on a unique journey, and we are all at different levels of spiritual development.

What if letting your individual light shine could empower humanity? What if you could become a co-creator with the universe and unleash unfettered development towards your highest self? What if that development could all flow from the journey you consciously chose to pursue? What if, in choosing to step outside of our comfort zone, we could usher in the challenges that would shatter the barriers to greater freedom, fulfillment, and joy?

Breaking down the walls in our minds is the very essence of freeing ourselves. But to get there we first have to recognize the powerful difference between our conscious and unconscious minds. Most of us have a misconception that consciousness just happens when our bodies are alert and functioning in our day-to-day lives. In fact, even in our waking lives, most people are driven almost entirely by what is already stored in our subconscious mind. However, the consciousness addressed in *Food Of the Spirit* is a realm of all possibility, connection to our source energy, and to the divine Creator which dwells within each of us. When we are awake in this real sense, we are powerful agents for change in our own lives, in the lives of those around us, and in the world. Each one of us possesses an energy that others can sense; it has a cumulative effect on the Earth, whether positive or negative. Because were designed to be in relationship, by making changes within ourselves, we can quickly change the world.

For years prior to making this shift, I thought I had things figured out. I didn't. To be candid, I still don't. Life is still presenting me with opportunities to learn and grow every single day. But this book is a collection of some of the most valuable things I've learned so far—things that have made a huge difference in my own life and that I want to share with you.

You are the secret. You only have to come alive. This book is precisely about coming alive and the learning opportunities that are there for you to embrace along the way—opportunities that may be hard to see at the moment.

The first step? Relax!

Many of the experiences I've had in recent years could never have been planned by me. They weren't some big effort on my part. Rather, they were divine appointments. The right people or circumstances were put in my path at exactly the right moment. It's hard to see them any other way. Each one of those experiences taught me something about myself and the world around me, facilitating healing and fostering growth.

Life is full of divine appointments. My hope is that this book will be one of those appointments for you.

Monkeys Hate Bananas

Life is 10% what happens to you and 90% how you react to it.

— Charles Swindoll

We constantly receive feedback from the world around us. Our physical senses take in information, process it and respond accordingly. From these indicators we conclude whether we live in a safe or hostile environment. We are all well aware of free will, our ability in each moment to direct our path in life. What we ponder on less are our automatic responses to the situations we encounter. We may not know why we respond in a particular manner, we just know that it is how we have always operated. Let's call these automatic response *programs*. Our programs, in fact, dictate, or drive, the decisions we make on a daily basis. Believe it or not, monkeys and bananas can shed a lot more light on this concept.

I once heard a story about a group of psychologists who set out to test the learned responses of monkeys. The story wasn't actually true. It's a pastiche. Some of the things to which it refers do indeed have a basis in fact, but the details have been significantly changed and embellished over time. Nevertheless, much like one of Aesop's fables, it is a great illustration of some important truths worth examining. Here's the story as it was told to me:

Five monkeys were initially observed in a controlled environment—a room with a ladder. At the top of the ladder hung a bunch of bananas. On the first day of the experiment, the monkeys all climbed the ladder to get the bananas. The scientists considered this normal behavior, noted it, and permitted it for a couple of days, uninterrupted.

After a few days, however, the scientists decided to spray the four monkeys at the bottom of the ladder with ice-cold water from a hose, while the monkey climbing the ladder was not sprayed. As one-by-one the monkeys would climb the ladder, this same process of spraying the monkeys at the bottom of the ladder was repeated.

A peculiar thing happened.

The monkeys learned quickly that they would be punished if any one of them tried to climb the ladder to the bananas. This negative reinforcement disincentivized the monkeys from climbing the ladder to retrieve the bananas. But the impact on the monkeys was even greater. When one of the monkeys would attempt to climb the ladder, the other monkeys would pull that monkey off the ladder and keep it from going near the bananas. Eventually, none of the monkeys would even go near the ladder.

This new behavior intrigued the scientists, so they removed one of the monkeys, exchanging it with a monkey new to the environment. They then performed one further phase of the study. With the new monkey introduced, the scientists opted not to spray the monkeys to deter them from climbing the ladder. Yet, when the new monkey tried to climb the ladder to reach the bananas, the other four monkeys would rally together to pull him off the ladder in full anticipation of being sprayed with cold water. Soon the new monkey wouldn't climb the ladder either.

The scientists continued to rotate the monkeys out one by one. Ultimately, the original test group had been completely replaced with five new monkeys, each which had never been sprayed with water but none of which would climb the ladder to get the bananas. None of the new monkeys ever knew why the other monkeys were pulling it off the ladder. Nevertheless, each learned from its peer group not to climb the ladder and retrieve the bananas.

The monkeys were *programmed* to respond to their environment. Through that programming, they lost their free will.

Free will, by definition, is the ability to make decisions without external coercion. When we say we have free will, we mean that we have control over our choices, what we do and how we react to any given circumstance.

Here's the difficulty, though. We believe that our conscious mind is in charge. But in reality, our programming—our subconscious—is actually primary. Exercising free will, then, means we must overcome our subconscious programming. Our situation may be the same, but our response can change. True free will, not just the illusion of it, requires some work on our part. But taking the time to do that work will be some of the most rewarding and liberating of your life.

The monkeys in the experiment ended up choosing not to go up the ladder to retrieve the bananas. Had they not been programmed, would they rather have climbed the ladder, so they could eat the delicious bananas? Of course! Programming ultimately overpowered their free will with the belief that they would be punished for attempting to do what they wanted and what they may even have had a biological imperative to do to survive! It's a powerful story, one that's regularly reflected in our everyday lives.

What is a belief and where does it originate?

A belief is simply a thought we keep on thinking.

This is why daily affirmations work. They often feel fake at first, because you don't believe them yet. However, persist with repeating a new thought over and over, and it will eventually feel familiar. Essentially, it can turn into a belief held as true. It's a powerful example of our ability to reprogram our subconscious mind with self-chosen beliefs.

What are some of your beliefs? You almost certainly hold some positive and some negative beliefs. On the positive side, for example, you may believe you are a gifted musician or a responsible citizen. On the negative side, you may believe you're not very likable or that others are always out to take advantage of you.

However, it turns out that many of our "beliefs" do not stem from our *own* choices and conclusions. In fact, we might immediately hear a parent's or teacher's voice when we begin to consider our beliefs closely.

So, there's another important matter to consider as we move toward greater free will in our thoughts and decision-making. As we begin to examine our beliefs more closely, it's worth it to ask ourselves in relationship to each of them: "Where did this belief come from? Who is my truth provider?" Doing so will go a long way toward sorting out which beliefs are true and potentially helpful to us and which ones are potentially false, requiring greater investigation and change.

Every day, the human brain is bombarded with so much information that much of what we do necessarily becomes an automatic response. As our physical body moves through an experience, our subconscious interprets our held thoughts and beliefs, most often triggering our automatic responses. Based on our subconscious programming we create the reality we expect and confirm the beliefs we choose to hold. This phenomenon is called *confirmation bias* and, while we're generally not aware of it, it drives most of our choices and behavior.

For example, in political races we tend to listen to those that agree with our beliefs and reinforce our thought patterns. We gravitate to those candidates whose rhetoric aligns most closely with our existing thought patterns. Listening to those with whom we agree and blocking out those with whom we do not is one means of confirming our existing biases.

The pitfall of confirmation bias, though, is that it tends to cause us to interpret new evidence or recall information in a way that confirms our existing beliefs even when that belief is not fact- or reality-based. As humans, we have a need to be right, to validate ourselves—and the stored information about who and what we are resides largely in our subconscious.

There's a second phenomenon that comes into play, as well. After an experience, we regularly engage in something called hindsight bias: We confirm to ourselves that what we thought was correct was indeed correct. Doing so solidifies even further the thoughts and beliefs we hold.

Have you ever been in a conversation with someone whose belief overrides the reality of objectivity? You could be talking about how beautiful the blue sky is and they insist the sky is orange. It's absurd and often frustrating from our perspective. You can see that the sky is, in fact, blue. What you don't see is the orange tinted glasses the other person is wearing. But for the other person, based on their subconscious programming and the way it is almost certainly being reinforced, the sky, along with everything else, is orange. This is reality as they understand and embrace it, so they will continue to argue for it.

The takeaway from this example? Our *perception* of reality plays a big role in the *outcome* of our reality.

Often we think that the problems we are dealing with are not our own but the result of another. Our disappointment and frustrations spring forth from unmet expectations. Yet, the easiest—perhaps the only—way to change others is to change ourselves. In point of fact, no two people see the exact same thing. Each of us interprets our surroundings based on what we currently hold and understand as truth. We make all of our decisions from this place of being— from the emotions we attach to our circumstances and what we deem to be in our best interests. In essence, whether consciously or unconsciously, we make decisions about what we actually can or should learn through the experiences we encounter.

The good news is, we can change our perception at any moment.

It's just like flipping through the channels on the television: you have control of the remote control. When a situation arises that is not conducive to your highest good, you have the ability to say, "I'm going to choose a different program."

Better still, miracles happen when you change the channel. There is a path of increasing order. If in every moment we choose to dissolve those specific automatic responses that do not serve us, we increase our freedom.

Like that mythical monkey experiment, we may not know why we do something in a certain way—just that we have always done it that way. The first step on the journey to greater personal freedom involves simply pausing to consider what currently held beliefs are in play. When a decision presents itself, step back for a moment and ask yourself two questions: first, "What are my beliefs in this moment? and second, "Do those beliefs serve me?" If they do, keep them. If they don't, determine to replace them. As we begin to analyze our options and the way our beliefs are impacting the decisions we make, we can take real and significant steps in redesigning our belief system and the way in which it drives us to respond to any given situation. With increased awareness and time, negative automatic impulses can be changed to positive ones. It's not so much that your subconscious will cease to function. It's more that, through conscious effort, the programming in your subconscious can be made to serve you better. You can take charge of ensuring that it enhances your freedom and choices rather than unnecessarily restricting them.

Are you ready to go deeper? Are you ready to absorb the next secrets in redesigning your beliefs and responding more freely to the situations you confront in your life? Are you ready for the incredible benefits that freedom will yield to you?

Keep reading…

Surrendering...Isn't for Sissies

Always say 'yes' to the present moment.
What could be more futile, more insane, than to create inner
resistance to what already is? What could be more insane
than to oppose life itself, which is now and always now?
Surrender to what is. Say 'yes' to life—and see how life
suddenly starts working for you rather than against you.
— Eckhart Tolle

It took less than 24 hours for my life to dramatically change. As I
sat contemplating what my life had been up until this point and
where I wanted to go from here I drew a blank. The night before, my
world had been rocked by a dream. At three in the morning, I was
awakened by an infusion of spiritual knowledge. My fiancé, partner
of almost five years, the man I was to marry one month from now,
had chosen another. In my dream, he had found someone else. What
we'd had would be no longer.

On awaking I tried calling him, no answer. I called his best friend
to be reassured that everything was okay, that I had simply had a
nightmare. When our mutual friend picked up the phone I blurted
out the question that expressed my fear: "Has he been seeing her?"
I named the girl that had showed up in my dream. But instead of
the reassurance I sought, this friend responded that it was not his
place to comment on what was going on. He wouldn't answer any

of my questions. He'd said almost nothing, yet I now knew all that I needed to know. Without directly expressing that the relationship was over, he had told me.

I hung up. It quickly sank in that our friend had known what was going on for some time. A few hours later my fiancé called and told me we needed to talk.

When he arrived he looked tired and a little beat up. I knew this moment must not be easy on him either. After all, he had been carrying around the knowledge that this difficult conversation was inevitable. Moreover, he was undoubtedly holding onto a sense of guilt. I, on the other hand, had thought everything was perfect during the last couple of months.

The first thing out of my fiancé's mouth was far from delicate. "I don't love you anymore, at least, not the way I should." I didn't know what to say, so I said nothing. I just sat in silence.

He continued. "I know we could have a happy life together. You'll be an amazing mother and helpmate." Was I hearing things? He was telling me that we had the perfect life ahead of us, yet he was choosing to jump into the unknown and give it all up anyway? I didn't understand. I still couldn't speak.

He kept talking. After I had called our mutual friend, that friend had called him, he told me. He wasn't sure how I knew who he was seeing. He said he tried very hard to protect me so that I wouldn't be hurt. It was bizarre to me that in order to protect me he hadn't told me the truth about what was happening. I had so many questions but stunned, like a deer in the headlights, I didn't ask any of them.

That day I learned a hard lesson in surrendering that which was not mine and that which I had no control.

You see, I had built my world around someone else. Along the way I had lost myself, the desire of doing for myself, and any idea of what I would do now that I was moving forward alone. I had always said that I loved his man more than anything, that his happiness was of the utmost importance to me. If that was true, then I had to support his decision, even though I didn't understand it at that moment. I got up and walked to the bathroom without saying a word. I took my ring off, gathered all the other jewelry he had given me, walked back to the living room, and gave them to him. For reasons I could not explain I was calm, peace had washed over me. I didn't cry or beg him to change his mind. I gave him a big hug and told him I loved him. With that he left.

For a while I sat in my oversized comfy, forest green armchair staring at the painting on my living room wall, thinking about nothing and everything all at once. I couldn't feel my body. I didn't feel heavy as one might expect. Maybe I was in shock. I remember thinking, "Why am I not crying right now? My world as I knew it is gone."

I picked up the phone and called my mom to let her know what had just happened. She was just as bewildered, and she was upset for me. It took me a good hour to convince her that she didn't need to call in to work to come see me for a couple of weeks. She was ready to hop in the car and make the 15-hour drive. Somehow, I reassured her I was fine. We agreed that I would call her right away if anything shifted.

I started making my way through the list of people that would need to be contacted, my bridesmaids, the church, the caterer, the photographer; so many people to inform that things had changed.

In church I had heard of "a peace that surpasses all understanding." This description fit me to a T in this circumstance. I certainly had some fear of the unknown. However, feeling the truth of the situation, I was acknowledging it and moving forward in-spite of it. Somehow, I knew it was right. I was surrendering to that which I could not change.

Surrender is an interesting concept. Think for a moment about what surrendering means to *you*. What is the first thing to come to mind? Is it defeat or waving the white flag? Do you associate surrender with relinquishing control or abandoning a piece of yourself?

Society has conjured up so many negative connotations around surrender. Yet, in fact, surrender is not at all about admitting defeat. In certain contexts, surrender can be a highly positive concept. In surrendering, we don't give up; rather, we open ourselves. Surrendering frees us from worldly circumstances that create chaos for our soul, yielding a place of growth. As we let go of how we believe things ought to be, we can more fully embrace that which awaits us, something far better and more perfect than what we have planned.

To put it mildly, surrendering can be uncomfortable. Yet, fear in these situations is actually alerting us that something important for our spiritual development is about to happen. The discomfort signals a decision point at which we have the opportunity to move beyond our previous limitations and experience growth.

There has been more than one circumstance in my life that humbled me to a place of surrender where I would not have ventured otherwise. Even with these circumstances, surrendering our plans seems scary. Without them, it often seems downright unthinkable. But in those circumstances, God was directing me to embrace the life which I was meant to live.

But how do you get past the fear?

The key to surrendering is trust—being certain of the outcome. God is always leading us down the right path. When my fiancé broke off our engagement, I could have lashed out and started yelling or sunk into a depression. Plenty of people would have understood and been supportive, but how would that have helped me or the situation? Instead, though I could not explain it at the time, I knew that this speed bump held for me the promise of much greater things to come. Trusting that my greatest good was being upheld, I was able to embrace the knowledge that I could navigate the stormy seas that would come.

I'm not talking about indifference, here. Surrendering definitely doesn't mean that you don't care what happens. Rather, surrender is, at its core, about letting go and letting God lead the way. As humans, we have limited perspective. Because God has a more expansive view and a bigger plan for you than you have for yourself—and because the universe has unlimited outlets through which to bless us—surrender, then, actually means caring even more that you are achieving the best possible outcomes for yourself and others. When you release the past that binds you, along with your expectations of the future, it frees up energy so that you can focus on being fully present.

To surrender we must let go of the need to control the situation and recognize that we simply don't have all the information we need. In fact, control in any given situation may not just be illusory but an actual illusion. To be sure, it has taken us a lifetime to learn our current patterns. But what do we gain by staying stuck? Surrender, then, is really a daily act that can be learned, becoming easier the more you practice it. Practicing it as a principle is liberating. As with anything, though, we need to learn how. Here are some things that I've found helpful in my own life.

I have a devotional time each day before my feet hit the floor. I start with gratitude, thanking my Creator for the day before me. Then I ask God for guidance: where he would have me go, what he would have me do, what he would have me say and to whom. I take a little time to hear what he has to say in response to these questions. As I allow myself to be still and get a sense of his answers, I then set my intentions for the day, being crystal clear and descriptive about them; what they look like, how they make me feel, how the actions I will take today move me closer to a particular end. Intention brings clarity and purpose to that which we are working to manifest. Clear intentions set the stage for our thoughts, feelings, and actions to propel us towards that which is already ours and surrender that which is not.

As powerful agents of change, it's crucial to be mindful of our thoughts in every circumstance. As we've already seen, thoughts repeated create our beliefs and the world as we understand it. Whether we interpret situations as good or bad is up to us. By being both mindful and intentional, we have the power to heal our life and surrender any situation to our greatest good. To that end, a great question to ask yourself in the face of any situation is: "How does the place in which I find myself facilitate my healing?"

We are not alone in this life, our Creator has gone before ensuring our path is magnificent; when we surrender we are able to follow the leader into the heart of the situation and its purpose to the truth. Everything we "need" is already available to us. Our journey is founded in teaching and being taught.

General rule of thumb: The more important something is to us, the more important it is to surrender it.

Worry robs us of our peace today, it can make us ill and kill the joy we could be experiencing in the moment. So, instead of giving in to worry, pray for peace. Place no stipulation on that peace, what it should look like, or the timing. Just be open to accepting God's perfect timing. When we look at life differently we experience life differently. A shift in perception is a miracle.

Dealing with this reality, and reacting to it, is perhaps one of the greatest challenges we face. It's also the key to our happiness, inner peace, and fulfillment. Learning to accept and welcome change is not just a daily commitment; it's also a life long journey. Each experience is an opportunity to explore further, to face our fears, to replace illusion with truth. Even what may seem to be the "wrong" decision is simply a different path.

When we believe that our greatest good will always prevail, we can walk with confidence, knowing that the tough times are merely life's preparation for the good that is to come.

Truth: You are continually being invited to take joy in the challenges you perceive.

Change Your Thoughts, Conquer Mountains

Everyone wants to live on top of the mountain, but all the
happiness and growth occurs while you're climbing it.

— Andy Rooney

I'm not sure how I talked myself into thinking it would be a good
idea to head off to the Middle-East with a guy I barely knew. Yet,
that was exactly what I was doing. I guess I must have figured that
if you want to get to know someone take a trip with them; from
which it logically follows that if you really want to know them take
a 3 month trip with them, in foreign, war-torn countries, without an
itinerary. What could possibly go wrong—other than everything?

Talk about testing your boundaries! I confess that the experience I'm
about to relay tested every emotion known to mankind. Whatever
expectations I may have had, I could never have predicted how much
I would learn about myself.

As we entered the war-torn countryside on the border of Turkey and
Iran, the breath was sucked out of my lungs like a vacuum had been
placed over my nose and mouth, then turned on high. I had spent
the last couple of days on trains, planes, and automobiles, traveling
half-way around the world to get here, to experience this moment, to

do something that scared me to death: to climb Mount Ararat, the tallest free-standing mountain in the world. Now, Ararat's rugged snow-capped peak pierced through the wispy clouds that danced on the bright blue canvas of the sky. Looking upon it, my heart seemed to stop, while all of time stood still.

We ventured down the dirt roads, rocks clicking against the metal undercarriage of the van, a billowing cloud of brown dust kicking up behind us. Small, rickety structures along the road appeared as though they were about to topple over from the sheer weight of the world around them. In the distance, my eye caught the image of a worn down building. Its paint was peeling away. Like everything else I was seeing, it seemed to be desperately attempting to distance itself from its own bullet-laden walls.

Our driver warned us we would be entering a dangerous region of Turkey called Kurdistan. The Kurd fighters called the PKK were actively trying to gain independence from Turkey, Iran, and Iraq. Not to worry, we had soldiers accompanying us to the base of the mountain. I looked at the others in the van; no one said a word. By the look on their faces I knew they were thinking exactly what I was: "What have I gotten myself into?"

The van came to a screeching halt jerking us forward in our seats, my seat belt tightened against my chest, yanking me back into the dirty and now slightly sweaty mesh seat. Three tanks surrounded us. My first thought? I can never tell Mom about this. She'd have a heart attack. With a tank in front of us, escorting us through the countryside and a tank on either side of our van we pressed onward to our goal, the mountain's summit.

The next few days were a blur. Unable to comprehend the stress I was placing on it, my mind went numb, locked into self-preservation mode. The biggest barricade between me and my goal was my own thoughts. But the only way I was going to get to the top of this almost 17,000 foot mountain was by placing one foot in front of the other. So, with the others in my group, I began.

As we marched forward, with a seemingly fearless leader who had ascended the mountain many times before, I expected to see desolate landscapes like those we drove through as we approached the base of the mountain. Instead, I was pleasantly surprised to find rolling hills full of sheep grazing on grass. In the distance we saw two men physically fighting near a donkey. Curious, and on high alert in relationship to my surroundings, I asked our guide what was happening. "They're fighting over who owns the donkey," he replied. Apparently, one of the men convinced that the other man's great-grandfather had stolen a donkey from his own grandfather, believed the donkey belonged to him. My guide said that the dispute was long-running and that they would still be fighting over the donkey for years to come. I was bewildered.

A small band of young boys from the ages of seven to nine were in the field tending sheep and protecting them from predators. Their presence broke my mind free from the conflict unfolding between the two men. When the boys noticed us coming, they ran to greet us. Their faces were marked with dirt, and their clothes were soiled as if they also slept with the sheep. They spoke no English, but with a smile and a nod they said in their native tongue, "Let us take this walk with you." They offered us walking sticks or homemade slingshots in exchange for whatever change we were carrying. I happily emptied the extra weight from my pocket in exchange for a homemade slingshot.

Our young guides.

As we approached the clearing, three young girls waited to offer us fresh sheep's milk. It was still warm. If I hadn't known any better, I would have thought the boy who'd sold me the slingshot had radioed ahead to his sisters to milk the sheep so that their traveling friends could have a refreshing drink as they journeyed along. The milk had an interesting texture and flavor to it. I humbly declined a second glass.

The girls that offered us a cup of fresh milk.

The children were full of life and ran circles around us giggling, until we came to the place where the clouds descended from the sky and met the path at our feet. The clouds were thick like fog, and stepping into them brought another dynamic to the mountain's mystery. As I walked through the clouds I almost forgot where I was, it was like being on another planet; when I came out on the other side, the peak of the mountain reappeared in grand stature. (We were still days from the summit.)

I was the only inexperienced climber on this trip, my colleagues consisted of men, all of whom had ascended some the highest, most dangerous mountains in the world, including Mount. Everest and Mount McKinley. They had lived to tell their stories, and I kept telling myself that I would too.

Waking every morning before the sun rose, we hiked all day long. At night, we would set up camp, then pass out—either from exhaustion or the lack of oxygen at the increasing elevation. Our tents were nestled between boulder fields in spaces almost too small for them. In the crisp air, each breath produced a puff of condensation that floated up from one's mouth only to bounce against the nylon of the tent and come falling back down on one's face as tiny snowflakes. As I went to sleep on the eve of our summit I heard the eerie sound of boulders breaking free from the mountain. In reality it had just been a massive pile of loose, crumbling rocks, but I was frightened, nevertheless.

"What are you thinking? You can't do this," I began to think to myself as doubts began to take hold. "You're going to die." My fears were creeping up, influencing my choices, keeping me from fully experiencing the summit. I knew that I needed to get a handle on my thoughts quickly.

While the situation I was in was more extreme than any I'd previously experienced, I also knew my own patterns and that I was falling into one of them. Negativity is one of the biggest obstacles I've had to overcome in my life. For most of my life, when I entered a new situation, my mind would first want to go to the negative possibilities, plaguing me with *'what ifs"* or *"what abouts."* Soon, I would find myself wrestling with self-doubt. I'd have to put my thoughts in a sort of head-lock and choke them out in order not to be crippled with ideas of what could potentially happen, when in fact, nothing had happened at all. By judging a situation before entering it, I was propelling myself away from rather than toward the magnificent life I was meant to live. I was keeping myself locked in a place of fear.

Today, those that know me well would say I have a happy, upbeat personality and that I generally focus on the good in situations. But it has taken time for me to come to this place. I used to live life with a preconceived notion of how things should work out, and in most situations, I believed I had figured out the best outcome. In reality, though, I was setting myself up for disappointment. A big piece of conquering the fear in my life has been to let go of expectations. More often than not, things do not work out exactly as we've planned. They certainly weren't working out that way for me. However, when things don't turn out exactly as we expect or wish, it does not mean they haven't worked out *perfectly*.

It turns out that, regardless of what I'd always thought, I didn't have the best sense as to what the optimal plan was. I also lacked the killer instincts I thought I had about what my greatest good was. When I began to let go of expectations—my attachment to specific outcomes—I became more and more open to the unexpected and *better* outcomes that any given situation held.

Of course, letting go in this way is often easier said than done.

Now, here I was, high up on Mount Ararat. If I was going to conquer my doubt and fear and make it to the summit, I needed to dissolve the barriers I had created to protect myself. I quite literally needed to make myself vulnerable to the greatness that awaited me. It was time to let go of my limiting beliefs.

But how?

If you're reading this book, then you have likely arrived at a similar, crucial juncture.

How we look at the circumstance we find ourselves in, and the expectations we assign to that perspective, definitely matters. If we expect the worst possible outcome in a situation that's difficult or uncomfortable for us, we're guaranteed to get it. If we focus on the good that can come from a challenging opportunity, that is what we will experience. This is the truth that I was beginning to grasp in a very real way: My life and the circumstances it encompassed was open to interpretation; I could choose a path that kept me afraid or one that would help me to grow.

As I faced my own tremendous challenge on Mount Ararat, as I sat with those negative thoughts and doubt creeping into my head, threatening to overwhelm me, I decided to pray.

Prayer is a a common thread woven through the tapestry of history. You can find it in every culture. Admittedly, different spiritual traditions have different ideas about what prayer is, what it looks like, how it works, and what it is meant to accomplish. But it's clear, even from research, that prayer has the ability to change the pattern of our brainwaves, mood, thoughts, and attitudes—or, in other terms, our energy.

Neuroscientist Dr. Andrew Newberg has been researching the link between the brain and religious experiences, such as prayer, since the early 1990s in an arena of study termed neurotheology. In his book *How God Changes Your Brain*, Newberg- reviews a vast amount of ongoing research.[1] The scientific evidence that has emerged points to the positive, long-lasting neurological effects of prayer and meditation on the body.

As we already know, thoughts have an impact on us. Just as toxic thoughts can cause adverse reactions to a person's mental and physical health, prayer can cause positive feedback mechanisms within the body. Dr. Newberg included subjects from multiple religious traditions in his studies, as well as different spiritual practices, including chanting and meditation. He found that the practice of praying changes the activity level of the brain allowing neurotransmitters in the brain to reshape the perception of circumstances. In the scientific world, such

---

[1] Andrew Newberg and Mark Robert Waldman, *How God Changes Your Brain: Breakthrough Findings from a Leading Neuroscientist* (New York: Balantine, 2010).

a shift is known as neuroplasticity. While many pray to influence their world, pleading for intervention or change, Newberg provides documentation that prayer is capable of changing us just as much or more then the world around us.

Whether you believe that prayer enables you to communicate more intimately with your Creator or simply connects you more deeply to your own spirit, there's clear evidence of its power. Newberg, then, has shown us an important bridge that connects our daily habit of praying to at least one key teaching in the Christian tradition. The Apostle Paul exhorts:

> "Do not be anxious about anything, but in every situation, by prayer and petition, with thanksgiving, present your requests to God. And the peace of God, which transcends all understanding, will guard your hearts and your minds in Christ Jesus."

> — Philippians 4:6-7 New International Version (NIV)

How much prayer are we talking about? Newberg's research suggests that, a mere twelve minutes a day of focused prayer over an eight week time frame resulted in measurable results that could be observed on brain scans.[2]

When I pray, I do so to free myself from fear of the outcome. The act of praying helps me remember that my greatest good will be served. We cannot bend the universe to our will. However, we can work with it. In prayer, we are not so much expecting or waiting for the world to change as we are shaping our position in relationship to any outcomes. The practice of prayer, then, amounts to consciously changing our world—our sphere of experience—by changing our thoughts.

---

[2] Ibid, pp. 26-27.

Since our beliefs are the thoughts we continually think, the longer we repeat a thought, the more tightly we will hold on to the resulting belief. It makes sense, then, doesn't it, how important it becomes to watch every thought? When you decide to take on this task, don't forget to pat yourself on the back when you begin to catch and correct yourself; it's an indication that you've truly begun to change your awareness and thought patterns and align to your highest truth. You don't have to believe everything you think.

I now make a habit of pausing and asking myself if my thoughts and beliefs serve me. If they do, I keep them. If they don't, through prayer, I search out what will. Remembering to pray, forming the habit of praying, can take time and practice, but the great thing about life is that it continually yields learning opportunities. Every circumstance is malleable when we realize that we can choose to see things differently, and prayer is one of the most powerful and dynamic tools we have to achieve that end. Like an onion, we can peel back the layers of our own thoughts and attitudes. As we peel off the old skin, the core is unveiled. The more we challenge ourselves to get to the core of our thought patterns, the more we can throw away the negativity, replant new seeds, and allow them to grow anew.

Our thoughts represent the state of our inner-consciousness. When we connect to our inner state of consciousness, when we go within to understand the core of any thought and its origins, we break the chains that bind us. We are capable of anything we put our minds to. The question is: Are you willing to stop beating yourself down by focusing on your limitations and instead realize that you are limitless—that you are capable of more than you give yourself credit for.

Another way to think about what prayer does for us is to visualize life as a giant, cosmic waterslide with many possible tracks. One track is the fastest, capable of bringing the most delight and excitement as we travel along it, before ultimately plunging into the pool of beautiful, cool, clear water at the bottom; all of the other paths to the bottom provide a very bumpy ride down, marring the experience. The choice of tracks is literally ours. Will we leverage prayer and awareness to create positive thoughts and reinforcement that allow us to slide into the life we are working to create? Or will we choose to hinder ourselves? By harnessing our thoughts we reframe our lives. In reforming our own lives, we naturally impact the lives of others and offer them the courage to reform their own lives.

But back to Mount Ararat. I had prayed. Now I needed to see what would unfold.

We woke at 3:00 a.m. that morning and began our expedition to the summit. I felt half-asleep, as if I'd been awakened by a rooster crowing before the first rays of the sun pierced the sky. Before leaving the warmth and relative safety of my sleeping bag, I bundled up in layers of clothes, then stepped outside the tent to find a sky crammed full of twinkling stars. Individually each star was a beacon. Together, they illuminated the landscape of the night. I thought to myself that, despite how many millions of stars resided in that sky, they weren't competing; they just shone gloriously because that is what they were created to do. They were there to remind us not only of the vast complex universe in which we live, but also the role we play in it. How perfect, I continued to reflect, since that is the exact reason each of us is here, to shine our light for all to witness.

It was time to grab hold of my thoughts and test myself. The man in the moon reflected his image back to me and, with his amber glow, seemed to be watching me, telling me that it would all be okay.

My first test came moments later. Our guide handed me an ice ax and crampons, then told me that if I slipped and began to fall off of the mountain, I should dig the pick into the snow and self-arrest. I assumed self-arrest meant save yourself from falling to a horribly brutal death by bouncing off the boulders on your way down the icy terrain. Not a pretty picture. I acknowledged my negative thinking and chose to see things differently. I thought to myself instead, "Wow, this ice ax will help me balance my footing on the climb. It's a valuable tool to have." With my headlamp lighting the way, I set out to reach the top of the mountain.

That day my chosen intention was to summit Mount Ararat. An icy wind blew off the mountain chilling me to the bone. My feet were sore from the two acclimatization hikes, and my legs were screaming that they couldn't take me any further. My mind was like London—foggy. The questions bombarding my brain created an opaque vapor that I had to keep working to clear away. Why had I undertaken this monumental and often grueling challenge? Why was I even awake at this insanely early hour? What dangers awaited me on the mountain? What had ever made me think that I could do something so crazy?

To combat these creeping thoughts and the doubt that accompanied them, I kept repeating to myself over and over again, like the little engine that could, "I think I can, I think I can, I know I can, I know I can." It sounds silly, but it helped. I was literally having to create a new foothold with every step, kicking my foot into the snow three times in order to dig out a stable platform in which to place my weight. My feet were in double plastic boots with crampons on the bottom. While they kept my feet from getting wet and increased my grip in the snow, they were incredibly heavy. Moreover, the thinness of the air at that altitude made me feel as though I was breathing through a straw.

It took hours to scale the last leg of the mountain. But the man in the moon continued to light the path until he finally gave way to the dawn. The sunrise began as a mere flicker of light dancing along the horizon, beckoning me to release the tension and enjoy the climb. The top of the mountain was now just a few hundred yards in front of me. I wanted to run to the top, but I stayed the course. I saw some of my teammates at the top, waving me onward. I couldn't help but smile. I had taken control of the fear that had urged me to quit. I had rejected the thoughts that didn't serve me. And now, here I was, at the summit of a mountain I'd once never have been able to imagine climbing.

Pursuing this challenge had served me in one of the best ways imaginable. It had brought me to a point where I didn't have the luxury to think negative, limiting thoughts about what I couldn't do. It required me simply to focus on what I *could* do. I had traveled halfway around the world, through war-torn countryside, and I had scaled one of the world's highest mountains. But what I'd actually scaled and conquered was the thoughts that had been paralyzing me—not only in the immediate situation but in my life as a whole.

To change my life, I had to start with things I was doing daily. In this respect, changing your own life will be no different for you. My patterns of negative thinking had followed me across the world. While it was the experience on Mount Ararat that provided my breakthrough to change, yours can be just as easily achieved at home. The choice is yours, whenever you wish to begin.

Our team atop Mount Ararat.

The Struggle Is Real, And It Heals

There is no learning without remembering.

— Socrates

I was amazed to realize how many historic biblical moments happened within walking distance of each other. I'm not sure why this was so surprising, logically, Israel, where so much Biblical history unfolded, is a relatively small landmass. The primary forms of transportation during Jesus' life were camels, donkeys, and walking. Looking out atop the Mount of Olives, one will view thousands of gravestones that date back centuries. And in the distance, just past the graves, is the Old City of Jerusalem. There, the Wailing Wall and the golden Dome of the Rock seems to sit peacefully amongst the growing commotion that encroaches.

On this trip I was fortunate to have an Israeli Christian Palestinian as my guide. In fact, this combination was important, because license plates in Israel are color-coded to indicate which areas a vehicle are permitted to enter. To be discovered driving through an area outside one's jurisdiction of clearance would mean big trouble. We needed someone who'd be able to take us into many different areas without a problem.

Our guide, Makhoul, showed us his driver's license. It listed his religious affiliation. While Israel has since changed its policies, I found this kind of public disclosure unsettling at the time. My mind began spinning into private thoughts about how intolerable such a mandate would be in the U.S. What was the purpose of having such information on a license? For what was the information used? I was having a hard time wrapping my mind around this bewildering discovery. If a person went to the store to purchase an item and were asked for ID at the register, would they be discriminated against or judged for their religious beliefs?

Makhoul was an excellent guide, very knowledgeable on the Bible and the history in the area. One night he invited us back to his home to celebrate his daughter's birthday. We gladly accepted. I love spending time with locals, and it was a rare opportunity to gain insight into Makhoul's life and a culture I desired to understand. My traveling companion, Joby, and I were already very fond of our guide. Meeting his family solidified our appreciation for our newfound friend.

On a daily basis, our experiences in Israel uncovered fascinating cultural traditions and differences that sometimes delighted us and, at other times, took us by surprise. In Tel Aviv, for example, Joby and I decided to visit a beach near our hotel one afternoon. Our outing was cut short, however, when we discovered that there were segregated areas for men and women. Unwilling to visit the beach separately, we decided on exploring the city streets instead.

In Jaffa, we visited the Wishing Bridge. Ancient legend holds that when a person steps out onto this bridge in faith, looks in the direction of the sea, and makes known their wish, they will find favor for the wish to become a reality. I took the chance the bridge offered. Stepping out onto the bridge, I made my desire known: I set the intention to make Joby my husband. In faith, I believed he would one day be.

Walking the time-worn street of Jerusalem, where the son of God had once carried the cross while crowds taunted him, shook both Joby and I to the core of our beings. Within timeworn Jerusalem, in the Christian Quarter of the Old City, is the Church of the Holy Sepulcher, where many historians believe Jesus' tomb was located. Others speculate that Jesus rose from the Garden Tomb, a theory that made the most sense to me. Visiting the holy sites where Jesus was said to have been both laid to rest and, three days later, rose again was a highlight of the trip.

The Garden Tomb where Jesus rose from the dead.

Bethlehem, Jesus' birthplace, is located in the Occupied Palestinian Territories. Israel controls all passage of people and goods in and out of the territories. Driving up to the entrance sent chills up my spine. A sterile concrete wall, 430 miles long and 26 feet tall, with metal barbwire on top and complete with lookout towers, armed guards watched over the coming and going 24 hours a day. It was creepy— reminiscent of a U.S. federal penitentiary. We were told to prepare our documents and exit the vehicle. Makhoul was to stay with the car. Three armed guards with fully automatic weapons began searching the car as we were swept away to a holding area. Once our car was cleared, we were moved through security, thoroughly searched, and then directed down a long brightly lit hallway. I began to wonder what had happened to our trusted guide and where we were headed. The end of the hallway brought us to a heavy reinforced steel door, followed by a roundabout that opened up on the other side of the wall. We hurriedly walked through, seeing our car and driver waiting for us on the street. Looking at the wall from this side we saw murals covering the concrete. One image has been forever burned into my mind. The artist had spray-painted a lion with snarling teeth biting into the back of a lamb. Around the image written in black letters and outlined in white were the words: "Let My People Go."

Not fully knowing what I was in for, we drove towards the center of Bethlehem. The media regularly portrays this area and the people that reside here as hostile. I reminded myself that the actions of a few should not speak for the population as a whole. People in every race, religion, and creed do horrible things to others. Yet, this place, which held so many of the sites important in the life and ministry of Christ, was different than the way I'd mostly been led by news reports to imagine it.

In the center of town, we saw people dressed up in their Sunday best, heading into church. We joined a congregation at the Church of the Nativity, built on the site where Jesus' birth is said to have occurred. They welcomed us with their smiles.

After the service we drove from Bethlehem through Gaza. Rockets were being shot overhead, and we saw buildings that had recently been hit. Even as a naïve traveler, I knew we were not safe here; yet, the strangest thing was occurring. It was like I was instantly transported to an alternate universe, one that the people walking down the streets found completely normal. Though war was waging around them, they went about their day as if nothing were amiss—walking their dogs, picking weeds in their front lawns, and talking to their neighbors. I felt a sense of fear wash over me and simultaneously I felt temporarily outside myself in utter disbelief. It felt like I had driven into an episode of the Twilight Zone, where the characters are unaware of how bizarre their lives have become to the outside world.

Judgement - versus Condemnation

At this point, I need to make an important differentiation between judgement and condemnation.

We navigate our day through the judgements we make. Judgements are decisions we make based on our opinions and we can judge in either a negative or a positive light. Through judgement we decide if we are safe. Judgment also enables us to determine if something is "right" or "wrong" based on the information we currently have stored in our subconscious.

Condemnation is instead what occurs when we negatively assess the values and behaviors of others. When we condemn, we take a judgement and leverage it to label another as wrong for their actions or behaviors. Condemnation regularly informs and impacts our perception of the situations in which we find ourselves, working to elevate us above others. Condemnation, then, edifies the ego at the expense of others.

Our ego will present itself time and again, challenging us to overcome it. Notice that the ego is loud. It shouts, vying for our attention, insisting that its commands be heard. It is sensitive to anything it perceives as a physical or emotional threat.

From our birth to the time of our death the world around us is working to mold what we think, say and do. One way we are conditioned in life is through fear. Fear, however, is not meant to hold us back in life; it provides an important signal, showing us where there is opportunity for our spiritual development to break through perceived limitations.

As we judge others, our fears are revealed. Fear can be thought of as an anagram:

False
Evidence
Appearing
Real

Fear is our emotional brain trying to take over, and it can sometimes take the rational brain a few seconds to catch up and take control. Often fear springs from the unknown, coaxing us to remain solidly within our comfort zone. Fear is the voice passing judgments about our circumstances and our position in relationship to them: "It's scary"; "I can't do it"; "I can't afford it"; "I don't know how." Rather than resisting what we do not want, the way out is to uplift and build what we *do* want.

There are some fundamental steps to working through nearly any fear:

1. Identify the negative thought, worry or heaviness.
2. Explore the basis for the fear.
3. Question whether the fear is real or perceived.
4. Take a mental step back to assess the situation and work toward a solution.
5. Release the fear and move on.

As we take control of our self-limiting beliefs we put the ego in check and change our feelings of worry, fear, anxiety, anger, condemnation, or righteousness, all of which result in perceptions of chaos.

Know that whether we reflect fear or love it is a choice we make. The result of building awareness around these two fundamental states and their influence on our perception is to honor our spirit. When we find ourselves in a situation that requires such a choice, will we stop, be mindful, and play out the situation before reacting? Will we give in to fear or trust the intuitive wisdom that guides us through fear into love?

Testing Borders

The border crossing into Jordan from Israel was a test of patience. New to international travel I had assumed incorrectly that crossing borders would always be an uncomplicated process. But now, what might elsewhere have taken less than an hour took us almost four hours. To make matters worse, we didn't want an Israeli stamp in our passports. We instead asked that a separate piece of paper be used and inserted into our passports. This request brought us into question. What many may not realize, though, is that there are other countries in the world that will deny you entry into their country if you have visited Israel. There was so much of the world we still wanted to see, and we didn't want to risk being turned away.

Once we made it through the border, we spotted a man in his forties with ruffled black hair, dressed in a clean, pressed, white-collared shirt, khaki pants and dress shoes, holding up a sign with our names on it—our Jordanian driver, who was waiting for us. On getting into his car, we discovered that he did not speak English and his name card identified that this was a new occupation for him. We endured a lurching ride in the back of the car, the driver perpetually stepping on the gas while simultaneously pumping the brakes. It felt like the car was doing a strange dance with the road. Only after several hours did we finally arrive at our destination, the Wadi Rum desert.

Aptly known as the Valley of the Moon, the Wadi Rum, is a vast expanse of desert where sandstone and granite rock transform arid land into a surprisingly hospitable place. Cultures have thrived there for centuries. In this remarkable place, Bedouin nomads invited us in for a cup of cinnamon tea. A canopy shaded us from the hot desert sun and the blistering blowing sand. Over an open, wood flame fire, a kettle heated while fresh cinnamon was ground. As we sat and waited, unable to communicate, I found that we didn't need words. Men from the tribe came back to the camp on their camels for an afternoon rest. Though, dusty and visibly tired, they did not rest; instead they brought out instruments to play for us, and we all danced together enjoying the moment.

Sipping cinnamon tea with the Bedouins.

Parting from our hosts, we then made our way to the Wadi Rum's hidden gem: the lost city of Petra, thought to have been built as early as the fifth century B.C. As we approached its entrance, we began to understand how this celebrated landmark could remain hidden for so long. Lost for years, it was rediscovered in 1812. The unassuming entrance could easily have been mistaken simply as a crack between two rocks. Yet, the small slit was deceptive. It twisted into and through the rose-colored sandstone, only then opening onto the a perfectly preserved, grand remnant of an ancient civilization.

We made our way through the site by camel. I was speechless the whole way. The mesmerizing architecture looked like it had once served as a home to giants. The entrance alone was a soaring 26 feet. But the temple itself measures an incredible 164 feet wide by 148 feet tall. Imagine a building almost fourteen stories tall, where the entrance is two stories tall. Those are the spatial proportions we were experiencing. I felt like an ant in the middle of it. Laborers had spent their entire lives dedicated to the completion of what we were witnessing. In order to carve this massive structure, workers had etched footholds into the rock; they had stood for hours, chiseling pillars and doorways in exceptionally brutal heat. The creativity of their hands and their dedication to the task transcended time.

The Treasury in Petra.

Unlike Makhoul our new guide was all business. At check-in, he warned us not to leave the hotel grounds, to keep our shades closed, and be aware of our surroundings. I figured it was standard procedure to keep guests clear of the fighting going on all around us.

That night at our hotel, unable to sleep, we pulled our mattresses off of the beds and out onto the deck. The heat of the day had worn off, and the cool desert evening was refreshing. The stars above twinkled as the full moon rose. Once again I was in awe of the greatness of God and the world he had created for us to experience. Laying there, I wondered what all the fighting was about. Did anyone really know? Couldn't we all just put aside the fighting, get along, and focus on innovating to make the world an even better place? Why was it so difficult to release the ego?

It's not quite that simple, of course. And yet, it could be.

Making Sense Of Established Patterns

Our brains learn through repetition and the establishment of patterns. These patterns enable us to respond quickly to the massive amount of information that comes at us from multiple sources. This is why we can drive home and not remember navigating there. Our brain simply relies on and activates our learned patterns.

Such patterns come into play in every area of our lives. In some cases they can be helpful. Yet, in other cases, the patterns we regularly leverage can be detrimental.

Two influences that can heavily influence the decisions we make are our emotional memories and our ego. When something that seems minuscule sets a person off in a fit of rage, an emotional memory is most likely influencing them. Once triggered, a chain reaction of behaviors unfold, usually without the person consciously thinking about what they are doing. They are, one might say, on autopilot. In general, past pain affects future response. So, if we do not engage in a process of healing the pain, we'll become stuck—much like those two men on Mount Ararat, still fighting that decades-long battle over a donkey.

We might compare the workings of the ego to a computer that operates based on a variety of programs. All programs run in accordance with the design of their creator. Either we create the programs we allow to run our lives, or we allow others around us to dictate those programs. Often the dominant program driving the ego involves a victim mindset. In this case, the ego rejects responsibility for its role in many—or even in *any*—situation.

When assessing a victim mentality, it may seem, on the surface, as if the "victim" is taking responsibility. In fact, though, holding a victim mentality often equates to a false state of responsibility. Though the victim role comes with certain perceived benefits, those benefits in fact turn out to be detrimental. A victim mentality, for instance, can lead a person into learned helplessness where no one expects them to take action, risk failure, or take any sort of personal responsibility. A victim mentality creates a false sense of pleasure by drawing attention and providing validation of the victimization. Though there are people who are victimized in this world, holding a victim mentality never brings about reconciliation or healing over time. Instead, it actually functions as a punishment to oneself and others. Perpetual victimhood can only prop up one's identity in a superficial and unsatisfying manner. Moreover, when other people get tired of the drama, the house of cards that the victim mentality creates is guaranteed to fall.

The ego attacks, manipulates, and works to solidify what it believes it must control. Yet, paradoxically, in a mental or emotional state of victimhood, we are, in reality, allowing ourselves to be controlled. This may be a hard statement to consider, particularly if you are currently in this situation. However, it's a very common and human situation for the grip of fear in our lives to control us. What is alarming is that people who live in a victim state are more likely to be victimized in the future. By allowing the ego to perpetuate fear and a victim state within us, we're actually putting ourselves at greater risk.

The question is always how to free ourselves of those talons that not only take hold in the ego but ultimately morph into impulses that are unhealthy and counterproductive for us. The aspects of ourselves that we work to suppress are, instead, the aspects we often most need to embrace and from which we have the most to learn. Actual victimization and perceived victimization are two very different things. A person can be a victim in a moment, a victim mentality however is a chosen persona, an image that is taken on for an extended period of time.

Let's be candid, being hurt sucks. That pain and the fear that becomes trapped with in it, will reveal your current expectations and values, showing you what you will—and won't—tolerate. This insight can make you a stronger person in the long run if you let it. For example, through the feeling of helplessness you can learn to take care of yourself instead of giving in to the role of being a victim. Through the feeling of having been used, you can learn to recognize your own great worth instead of embracing the pattern of your own exploitation. Out of having been abused, you can develop compassion. From feeling stuck, you can realize there is always a choice.

The way others behave in any given situation can confuse matters and make it harder to recognize truth. Always remember, though, that the way people treat you is a statement about the person they are, *not* a statement about you. Only the-way *you* react is a statement about you.

The perception that things are *wrong* or not turning out as they *should*, is a control mechanism. As we look through the lens of our programs, most of life is viewed in terms of only right or wrong— whether it turns out as it should or shouldn't; it's all about perception. When we allow our expectations to dictate our experience, we taint what could come from that experience. When we let go of expectations and live in the moment, everything just *is*.

What would happen if you simply took a mental note, a moment to process the situation, and then chose to respond to a given situation differently—if, for example, you consciously decided to refrain from getting upset with people or situations? Both, in fact, are powerless without your reaction. Being upset occurs when we take things personally or give them unwarranted life in our experience. If we take the outlook that things are what they are and nothing more, we free ourselves from attachment to the outcome—and inevitable fear and disappointment.

The ego is not inherently bad. Instead of viewing the ego as evil choose to see it as a check in balance system. Again, it's providing us with an important signal. Frequently, the loud voice of the ego is yielding a clear indication that we're not acting in love and kindness. The question is, will we embrace the signals it provides? When the ego speaks, we have a golden opportunity to ask ourselves a key question: "What do I need to learn in this moment?"

How we treat others creates our experience and a feeling of heaven or hell. The ego thrives on condemnation. We judge ourselves; we judge others; and we judge our worth in comparison to others. But when we're aware that everything we do is either healing us or taking us further from our truth, we can instantly alleviate a conflict by bestowing love on ourselves and others. As we choose to act in love, we untie the knots that bind us.

The Ego Has Many Faces

We recognize the ego's presence by the terms "I", "me", "mine."

When the ego is unhealthy or damaged it can lead us into some troubling thoughts and behavior. When our ego has sustained damage, it can insist that we are *always* more special and important than our brother. This tendency can lead us to deny personal responsibility and slough it off to others. On the other hand, there is such a thing as enlightened self-interest. This principle works to preserve our best interest and keeps us from being taken advantage of by others, all while promoting the best interest of everyone involved. This way of thinking brings about win-win situations in life.

The unhealthy, damaged ego tends to deal with states of lack through manifestations of want. It can also inauthentically equate our importance with an accumulation of material possessions. Our self worth never has, nor ever will, come from stuff.

Truth: As a child of God we can want for nothing for God has given us an identity, a mission, and everything that we need to live and achieve. Our job is simply to seek his will and make ourselves open to the ways in which he wants to accomplish it. We have the ability in every moment to change our outlook on life and what we get from it.

What is this moment telling you about yourself? You're already creating your reality. Is it the reality you want to experience? If not, isn't it time to figure out why you've created it the way you have?

For many years I struggled needlessly. I was notorious for replaying over and over in my mind any upsetting situations that would befall me. I continually magnified my emotions, perpetuating the negative response, making the circumstances more and more upsetting. I self-destructively tortured myself and almost certainly others around me as I shunted my own responsibility and blamed outside forces.

After years of playing out this unhealthy pattern, I realized that I was disempowering and hurting myself. I had to stop and ask myself, "Is that what I really want?"

When I took a moment to evaluate my contribution to the situation I noticed that, often, the person I was blaming for my unhappiness may not even have known that their actions had upset me. In some cases my distress resulted because I had perceived the situation in an unintended way. To escape this negative spiral, I had to shift my thinking so that I could see through the other person's eyes or from another outside angle.

By shifting the focus from myself to other people or situations and engaging in a blame game, I was empowering my ego in ways that kept me from addressing those aspects of a situation over which I actually did have control. It sounds odd perhaps, I finally had to recognize that when I felt others were mistreating me, my best bet was not to expect them to treat me better but to find ways to start treating myself better instead.

Life doesn't have to be a battlefield. It's okay to lay down the armor. I've learned that identifying fear, damage to the ego and our condemning human nature allows us to detach from that negative outcome and embrace the loving and forgiving, nature of God. My motto now is: Be kind, forgive, and move on. How other people treat us doesn't matter. What does matter—the *only* thing that matters, really—is how we respond. Treating everyone with love and respect reflects our character. Encountering the ego in ourselves and others gives us the opportunity to love others where they are. In moments of conflict, realize that what we're experiencing from another right now is not necessarily their true spirit, but may, in fact, be the result of a damaged ego. Healing the ego is a lifelong process. So is discerning and making the best choices out of the signals the ego continually sends us. But God can teach us to see ourselves and others as he does—if we let him.

When we acknowledge our wounds we can conquer them relinquishing their power over us in the present moment. Otherwise, we may project past hurts into our present moment, inhibiting the healing process. The key is to look at only the facts. Rational reflection can clear a space for emotional healing and gives us a framework to see the situation as it is. Once we have a clear space, the heart can then guide us to what is true. When we identify an old pattern and work through it, we serve ourselves and awaken the soul to solve a problem or situation, a higher level of thinking is required than the one that created it.

How To React Without Reacting...The Non-Reaction Method

The next time you feel your emotional state escalating, try a method called "non-reaction." Simply stated, non-reaction acknowledges that different people, groups or cultures process situations by different standards. What may be socially acceptable in one social or cultural arena may not be deemed appropriate in another. To fully understand any given situation, we must be willing to look at the circumstances through another's eyes. This practice is where our ego can help empower our greatest good and foster the greatest degree of peace, increasing the opportunity to move through the situation in a more healing manner.

If we indeed allow the ego to serve as a feedback system that positively supports, we can achieve three things:

1. remember consistently who and what we truly are;
2. keep an open heart; and
3. learn from each experience that presents itself.

Our feelings, thoughts, expectations, and experiences can all change daily. If we're not careful and rooted in a strong belief system, our sense of self, our perceptions of who we *are* can change right along with these variables. The ability to convey feelings, thoughts, or expectations begins with looking at the strong roots that lay our life's foundation. The gut feelings and physical reactions we have to a situation before us are necessary in our decision making process. However, they do not have to dictate our immediate response.

We process the world around us through our beliefs and perceptions. In this world not everyone shares our views. From a psychological perspective, we could view the ego as a one-sided attempt, through confirmation bias, to steer our decision-making process in a particular direction. Yet, as reasoning beings, we are better served by exploratory thought, where we consider alternative points of view and come to a conclusion after taking evidence and beliefs into account. Part of our human nature is the fabrication of explanations or stories that justify the behavior or actions which we choose to take. What we would otherwise deem good or bad, right or wrong, can change via the constant feedback of self-analysis or through social persuasion.

We become even more critical about our decisions and actions when we know we'll be held accountable. A spectrum exists across different cultures as to what is or is not acceptable. The beliefs we hold in our own culture typically become the standard by which we hold others accountable, even if it is not the same standard by which they hold themselves accountable. Certainly, different cultures and religions hold differing value systems regarding morals and ethics— what might be considered the individual's framework for deeming an action right or wrong. To be clear, I'm not talking about moral relativism, which considers that no one is ever truly right or wrong. There are, in fact, foundational, universal moral truths, and it's crucial that we leverage these as our guidelines.[3]

---

[3] To read more extensively on this topic, see:
Andrew Wilson (ed.), *World Scripture: A Comparative Anthology of Sacred Texts* (St. Paul, MN: Paragon House, 1991); and Richard T. Kinnier, Jerry L. Kernes, and Therese M. Dautheribes, "A Short List of Universal Moral Values, *Counseling and Values* (October 2000 Volume 45), http://personal.tcu.edu/pwitt/universal%20values.pdf.

The Golden Rule—"Do unto others as you would have them do onto you"—can be seen as a universal moral precept that transcends, race, culture, or religion.

Another precept that transcends race, culture and religion is the Non Aggression Principle, or NAP for short. Similar to the Golden Rule, NAP states that there are actions for which we are personally accountable and provides a general guideline on how to treat others. Based on the notion of treating others fairly—with dignity, equality, and respect—it specifically disallows the use of force, fraud or coercion to get one's way. For example, if I wanted your hat, I would not take it, unless you gave it to me, because otherwise I would be violating the prohibition against theft because I would not want you stealing my hat. In fact, it's hard, isn't it, to imagine anyone taking kindly to someone stealing from them, manipulating them, or otherwise forcing them to do things against their will? That's what makes NAP universal in nature.

The International Religious Foundation similarly leverages far-reaching ideals and codes of behavior. Its publication *World Scripture: A Comparative Anthology of Sacred Texts,* reaffirms the Golden Rule. It rejects what most of us consider the major sins of murder, theft, dishonesty and hypocrisy, while affirming the universal principles of justice, compassion, and forgiveness.

In living within these guidelines, it is not our place to condemn people. We make *judgments* daily, based on whether certain actions align with universal moral truths. To be clear, however, we judge behavior alone, rather than condemning the person engaging in the behavior. Only God can judge. Rather, we simply need to embrace the courage to accept responsibility and accountability for our own actions. Jesus expresses this principle perfectly in the New Testament, Matthew 7:3-4:

Why do you look at the speck of sawdust in your brother's eye and pay no attention to the plank in your own eye? How can you say to your brother, 'Let me take the speck out of your eye,' when all the time there is a plank in your own eye?

— New International Version (NIV)

Regardless of one's religious convictions or affiliations, it's difficult not to see the wisdom in this passage.

When we choose to change ourselves, we release the need to condemn or change others. We not only allow the people with whom we come into contact to be who they are, we extend peace, compassion, and love to them. The more we engage this practice, the easier it becomes. We don't have to agree with the behavior of others to bless and release them.

It's not just others who gain from our choosing to bless rather than condemn. We benefit as well. When we release the compulsion to condemn or change others, when we choose instead to focus on our own journey, healing takes place within *us*. It is always in focusing on our own healing, in fact, that we make truly extraordinary strides.

While it might not seem obvious, the way we think about others— the way we judge them—is deeply tied to our own sense of self.

As we've already seen, our perceptions of ourselves are forged early in our lives, forming a foundation. The experiences we continue to have as we go through life, either build upon that foundation or demand that we alter it.

Putting God's wisdom into action in our lives builds on a solid foundation.

The New Testament gives us a further glimpse into how we build a solid foundation:

> Command them to do good, to be rich in good deeds, and to be generous and willing to share. In this way they will lay up treasure for themselves as a firm foundation for the coming age, so that they may take hold of the life that is truly life.

— 1 Timothy 6:18-19 New International Version (NIV)

Let's face it, the unexpected and the unfamiliar are around every corner. But if we're so wrapped up in a damaged or dysfunctional sense of self that our only instinct is to be critical of the people and situations we encounter, what opportunity do we truly allow ourselves to move past our fear? If we can't find a way to remain open, how can we possibly establish a spiritual environment in which we can learn, grow, and benefit from the surprises life continually brings? While we may be in a birdcage right now, we have the power to open it from the inside. No one else, in fact, has that ability.

Non-reaction allows us to take a valuable step back to become an observer, if even just for a moment. It takes us temporarily out of the equation, giving us the opportunity to see perspectives outside of our own and draw in something other—perhaps higher —than ourselves. In doing so, we have a chance to realize that, except in very rare situations, no person or situation is an enemy to us. Each situation simply presents a learning opportunity capable of helping us to overcome our fears, rather than being ruled by them. Again, often the physical indicators of fear or tension simply serve as signals that something important to our spiritual development is about to happen, that we have a priceless opportunity to expand beyond previous limitations. When it comes to fear, our best way forward is to acknowledge the feeling without identifying with it and allow the spiritual opportunities and gifts that lie hidden in the situation to unfold.

Maya Angelou said, "Hope and fear cannot occupy the same space at the same time. Invite one to stay." Which will you invite to stay? If you are ready to release the fear, let's keep going.

Stop To T.H.I.N.K.

Our greatness lies not so much in being able to remake
the world as being able to remake ourselves.

— Mahatma Gandhi

Traveling the world, I've sat in the favelas of South America,
orphanages in Mexico, and with the homeless in America. At
another time or place, any one of us could find ourselves in similar
dire situations. There are many circumstances that bring people to
the places in which they find themselves. When we stop assuming
we know why each person finds him- or herself in their current
difficulties, we open the door to possibility and solutions. Instead of
wasting time on condemning others, we can instead spend our brain
power and energies in figuring out how we can help to better things.

My husband Joby and I have been on a mission to feed the five million
children who are dying worldwide each year from malnutrition. It
has been eye-opening to spend time with these children. When we
go to an orphanage, we make it our goal to offer constant nutritional
support to the children, to teach them how to cultivate food and
prepare it. The icing on the cake is that we are able to spend time
with them doing puppet shows, playing games, and loving them.

Teaching the children about nutrition.

On one of our best trips, we headed into the jungle of Cambodia to see how one village was changing their situation and visitors perceptions. Cambodia is considered a third world country, most of the population gets by on less than a dollar a day. Despite this poverty, the people were friendly and accommodating. When we arrived in Cambodia, we were taken back in time. Though some people had cars, horses and donkeys were the primary means for pulling carts through the streets. Our hotel cost less than ten U. S. dollars a night, which we later found out we could have gotten for half that price. A five star dinner was two dollars, and an hour-long massage was offered for between one and three dollars. A big part of what keeps the economy going is an influx of tourism, with Angkor Wat becoming the biggest draw since UNESCO named it a World Heritage Site.

Angkor Wat translates as "Temple City." The architecture is incredible. The ancient complex includes over 300 monuments built with five to ten million sandstone blocks, some weighing more than 3,300 pounds. Our guide informed us that this rock had been excavated in the twelfth century from quarries 22 to 54 miles away, then barged on canals through the jungle. Looking over the vast landscape I wondered to myself, "How was this mammoth feat possible without modern machinery?" I could understand how we could harvest the massive stone from the ground in the modern day, lift it with a giant crane onto the back of semi-trailers, and drive it the many miles from there to here. But the intricate system the natives had concocted to make this ingenious place a reality was mind-blowing. In the middle of a jungle, they built the largest religious monument in the world.

Near Tonle Sap Lake, we boarded a tiny rickety boat pieced together with half rotten scraps of wood. I wasn't sure it would float. It actually looked as if it might sink into the brown, murky water below. We motored along the waterways, passing children as they navigated the water in aluminum pots, steering their vessels with long wooden sticks with which they pushed themselves in the direction they were headed. We also saw small, floating shacks, mounted on big plastic barrels and stitched together with a multitude of textiles. One wall would be made of wood, while another was fitted together from pieces of plastic.

As we got closer to our destination, hundreds of these floating houses came into view; the village was much larger than I had anticipated. Children sprang from their front doors, tucking their knees to their chests as they leapt into the water, in true cannonball fashion. As they hit the surface, dingy water would burst into the sky, splattering anyone in its path. The laughter echoed off the water, spreading to contagion, and soon everyone in earshot was looking down the river laughing. A woman in a paddleboat, wearing a conical woven-reed hat, plucked leaves from a bush growing out of the middle of the water.

Our boat bumped into the dock of the school house, stirring my thoughts. With laser focus, the children were fixated on the lesson at hand, learning everything that they could, taking pride in their education. It was a privilege to attend. The lunchroom was an extension of the classroom, where rice and entrails were being prepared. The community did not have much in the way of material possessions. However, it was clear they were thriving. Locals with boats offered tours to the village in exchange for donations. Villagers were selling homemade goods, and a boy not older then five offered us the opportunity to take a picture with his pet snake in exchange for whatever change we had in our pockets.

The snake charmer.

This group of people, who would be judged as poor by society's standards, were rich in happiness, love, and resources. They had learned to work together, pool resources, share skill sets, to laugh, entertain, and love their neighbors. They trusted that what they had was enough. They chose to see their blessings. They had abundance according to their own definition. Their souls shined for all to see. Visiting their community blessed us beyond measure.

The community was living in what would be considered extreme poverty. Sanitation and clean running water were nonexistent. From another boat I heard a group talking about the living conditions and people in a negative light. It seemed unneeded, unwarranted. Honestly, it pierced and saddened me.

I do not think that the people in the other boat meant to be mean-hearted, they could simply have been processing the situation out loud as they perceived it, in the context of their reality—what they knew and not as a visitor, there to experience a different way of life.

Yet, our spoken words hold power and energy. Once we've sent them out, we can never take them back. When this truth finally clicked for me, I began catching myself, realizing that not every thought that came into my mind needed to be verbalized. It represented a path of true growth in my life, once I understood that holding certain thoughts back could actually prevent unintended damage.

I also discovered the importance of active listening, which has since served me incredibly well in dialogue with others. In active listening we invest the time to hear what another is saying to us, waiting to formulate our response until they have finished speaking. In addition, before we reply, we take a moment to consider what they have just said.

Too often active listening does not happen. We half listen to what is being said and begin to respond even before the other person has had a chance to finish their thought. Active listening takes practice. It helps us discern facts and better understand the people we are with.

Having been out of my own comfort zone more times then I can count I've come to rely on a valuable filter before speaking. It's easy to remember: T.H.I.N.K. before you speak.

T - Is it true?
H - Is it helpful?
I - Is it inspiring?
N - Is it necessary?
K - Is it kind?

Since embracing this filter, I've found that, I've been better able to let go of condemnation and its unproductive and even damaging outcomes.

Everyone has a role to play in the drama we call life; but that role, played out in the here and now, is only a blink in the grand scheme of things. Within each of us, at any given moment, lies the ability to rise to our-highest potential or to sink into the depths of despair. It is not our responsibility to judge others for where they are in their journey. In fact, we don't know what they've been through, what they may have been taught, the lessons they have yet to learn, or the greatness that will unfold for them in their own next chapter. The truth is that when we condemn another, something inside of *us* has been triggered; we're therefore frequently revealing far more about ourselves than we are about the other person. So, when we notice we're engaging in this sort of behavior, it's wise to pause and ask what it is about ourselves that we see being reflected as we confront that person or situation.

For example, a lot of judgement tends to creep in when we speak to segments of the population that live in a state of lack. The fact is, we live in a hurting world. But that same world encourages us to focus on what separates us from others and boast about what we have over them. So, while many of us are willing to give of our time and resources to help those less fortunate then ourselves, too often we're unwittingly looking down on our brothers and sisters, judging them on things that don't actually matter at the same time we're attempting to assist them. In this way, placing judgement perpetuates fear and division, which we already know actually hurts us and those around us.

Every quality we see in others exists in us. The information we are faced with is a feedback mechanism. When we notice that incoming information is affecting us, working through the steps outlined earlier, in order better to access and deal with fear, can make all the difference. Unless you find a way to rest with what you find yourself resisting, it will persist.

Going back to that Cambodian village, the truth was that these were beautiful, creative people who were working together to create a life that they loved and of which they were proud. To be helpful, we could bring resources and skills to empower, encourage, or even inspire them on their journey. Inspiration, though, is a two-way street. Our coming as foreign visitors with resources to offer may have inspired the Cambodians we met to do more for each other, see beyond their current situation to what could be, or any number of other possibilities. In turn, the people living on Tonle Sap Lake inspired me to do more, to be thankful and grateful. Sometimes the people we believe we are going to assist end up helping us by giving us much more than we could ever have given them. This was easily the experience we had in Cambodia.

The kindest thing — the most enlightened way to live — is to love each other right where we are, just *as* we are.

The Hearts Energy

Peace is the result of retraining your mind to process
life as it is, rather than as you think it should be.

— Wayne Dyer

Our heart is the first organ to develop in utero. The heart is our life
force; when it stops, we do also. To me this is not coincidental to the
fact that we are to live a heart-centered life.

Living a heart-centered life is safe, it's comfortable, it's living in love,
it's how we aspire to live. In order to live in this state of being we
must first take risks, to step out of our comfort zone. Of course, we
can all agree that risk feels neither safe nor comfortable. In taking
those necessary risks, though, we can still act in love, as living in
love never needs to be excluded from any scenario.

How can this be? How do we resolve this paradox of comfort co-
existing with discomfort?

The truth is that we were designed with a remarkable mind-heart
connection; the two are not exclusive of each other but are, in fact,
meant to work together. In communication with the Creator, for
instance, we use the feedback of the mind in conjunction with the
heart to discern the right path. As we discern this path, facts are
revealed as indisputable. Feelings become the signposts we've talked

about, the ones that direct us along the path of life—messengers that, if we listen, show us where we need to go and help us grow *through* our discomfort.

Experiential learning is invaluable in achieving a heart-centered life. One of the most transformational experiences I have had is working with hospice patients. Hospice is a special program reserved only for medical patients who have six months or less of life remaining.

Two individuals, in particular, bestowed lessons that changed my outlook on life forever. I call them my angels, because, despite the fact that they had "nothing left to offer," the wisdom they acquired and imparted as their souls journeyed onward impacted my life in ways that they will never know in this life. With great fortitude, they each endured the dying process, contributing to my growth by speaking from their heart to mine, telling me not what I wanted to hear but rather what I needed to hear. Their respective encounters, and the insight they were able to share with me, are incredibly valuable here.

From a very young age I knew I wanted to be a doctor. In my childhood games of let's pretend, I would help heal the world, creating a better quality of life for all. From the time I was eight, I not only knew exactly which school I wanted to attend to achieve that dream but also what I needed to do to get into that school.

I didn't really have to work hard in school; it came easily to me, and I enjoyed it. I had enough credits to graduate high school early, and the high school I attended offered an early enrollment program that allowed me to attend community college to earn college credit once my high school curriculum was complete. In my senior year of high school, I actually did earn my degree as a certified nursing assistant, or C.N.A., during which I learned techniques and procedures to help patients in the recovery process. In essence, I became a liaison between my assigned patients and the nurses.

When it came time to do my practicum, I was placed in a nursing home to work with hospice patients. It was one of the toughest jobs I have ever had. I wanted to think that my role conferred upon me the status of a mature adult, but I was really still just a teenager learning about some of the most difficult challenges and hardships of life. Of course, if I was looking for lessons that would help me toward true maturity, working in the hospice field was like getting thrown into the deep end of the pool. At my tender age, the experience taught me the invaluable lesson that none of us is promised to live into old age—that we have to treat each day as if it may be our last and that nothing matters more than living from the heart.

My patients were amazing and always thankful for the assistance I was able to offer them. More then providing them with physical care, though, my job involved serving as a professional listener. I heard countless stories from my patient's lives. As I listened to them, I had a closeup view to the deterioration of their bodies. Sometimes that deterioration would take place somewhat slowly, over the course of months. Sometimes it would occur in just weeks or days. My focus was to ensure they each knew they were heard and that their discomforts were eased to the best of my ability. One of my favorite patients, an elderly man named Melvin, was short and round with two wiry hairs about 6 inches long growing from the center of his balding head. He wore thin brown rimmed glasses and had maintained all of his faculties. In and out of hospice, I met Melvin during his second stint in the program. I quickly discovered that he had a strong will to live, which I believe he'd always had; he was fighting the cancer that was consuming his body, determined not to give in. In fact, when I first met Melvin, he had so much life in him that I would not have thought he was a candidate for hospice.

As Melvin began to share his stories, with me, I not only gained an understanding of his struggles and triumphs but also crucial life insights. Drafted into World War II, Melvin had a strong sense of duty to protect his family, his country, and future generations. But, as a veteran with firsthand experience, he didn't much like the idea of war—of impeding on and killing each other.

When he left for the front lines, Melvin had had to leave the lady he loved behind, not knowing if he would return. When he recounted these stories, his voice would crack, his eyes would begin to water, and his hands would sometimes begin to shake as he was transported in heart and mind to that traumatic chapter in his life. While he was serving, he met another young lady who helped him make it through his tour. Without my having to ask, I could tell that his feelings for this second woman were also still powerful.

Heading home from combat, Melvin had hoped to transition back to his previous life, which no longer meshed easily with his experience. Everything that he expected to be normal, familiar, and safe seemed foreign, and he was plagued by nightmares. He had killed many people, a reality that sat heavy on his heart. He'd walked off a foreign battlefield and onto a personal one, fighting to reconcile his military mission with his personal values.

At home, Melvin had searched to find his purpose, where he now fit in society. Stateside, his community saw him as a hero. Yet, he thought of himself much differently. A man of strong conviction, he also possessed and led with a tender heart. "No matter how big we think the world is, everyone is fundamentally the same," Melvin would tell me again and again. "We all desire to be loved and accepted and to have someone to share life's experiences with."

Eventually, the cancer overcame Melvin, and once it did, he headed downhill quickly. One Tuesday afternoon, he seemed extra tired while I was visiting with him. When I returned on Thursday, he was gone. I can't describe the sad, sinking feeling I had in learning that I had heard all the stories I would ever hear from Melvin. But the measure of what he had given me in the time I'd known him—the ways he'd helped me to understand what it meant to live a life of the heart—was already so much, and I still carry it all with me today.

Violet was the second person to whom I attended, a home care patient, who lived in a penthouse apartment that overlooked the city. Small of stature, she always looked immaculate—not a hair out of place. When I met Violet, she was dressed in a light pink twill jacket with matching skirt, a pearl necklace and earrings, sheer stockings, and matching orthopedic shoes. If someone was not doing her makeup for her every day, she was certainly doing an expert job of doing it on her own. She would sit in an oversized velvet chair, surrounded by art that was almost certainly part of a family collection and antiques that gave her home a museum-like quality.

Violet had been the perfect daughter for her aristocratic parents. An only child, there had been high expectations for her. Though she'd wanted to be a dancer, her parents had forbidden her this dream. Instead she did what was expected: she married a man her father had chosen for her. Pre-arranged marriage was common then, she told me, and she'd been reminded again and again that there was a legacy to uphold.

But Violet struggled. In talking with me, she expressed heartfelt sorrow that she'd never taken the opportunity to indulge her authentic self, because her whole life had been so wrapped up in what others thought about her—and in the then-accepted notion that women were not to speak their minds. If she just kept up the exterior beauty, she told herself, she would have value. She coped by telling herself again and again how privileged she was to live a life of luxury, but she never pursued her own dreams, instead putting them aside in order to be the person society and her family told her she had to be. Certainly, she didn't have a bad life; but she regretted not living the life she wished for herself.

Despite her regrets, Violet made a remarkable discovery late in life that she was able to share with me. "Inherently," she told me, "we are all perfect. We do not have to strive to be perfect, we were created that way." Physical beauty, she explained is fleeting; it is our character that matters and from which true beauty originates. "Always go after your dreams," Violet exhorted to me, "and live with a grateful heart." If that's not hard-won, heart-centered thinking, I don't know what is.

I admit that the thought of death and dying was very scary for me for a long time. It was in talking to Melvin, Violet, and many others, though, that I finally came to a crucial realization. We are faced with many small "deaths" all along life's way. While we do finally lose loved ones physically, we also lose people—and sometimes even ourselves—through broken relationships, lost jobs, declines in health or ability. These small deaths offer us opportunities to learn and prepare for the ultimate transition. They offer multiple chances to unseat our unconscious fears and show up for life fully.

Unfortunately, society has moved us away from heart-centered living. Following one's own heart and instincts is less and less encouraged. Instead most of us end up suspended in a state that leaves us easily influenced and led by social suggestion. We mostly do as we're told. We too often reject the light that divine guidance provides to us and shines on our path via the heart.

Our heart knows what our mind does not. It views reality outside time in a place of direct connection to our Creator and true self, permitting us to tap into inspired knowledge and insight that gives us a view onto reality in its purest form. So, in listening to our heart, we will never easily be led astray.

Living from the heart allows a radiant flow of energy to encompass our being and enables us to see the hearts of others. Again, it allows the natural connection of our heart and our head to work as designed.

As graduation grew nearer, my time with the hospice program came to an end. I was still headed toward that dream of being a doctor, right down to the institution I'd chosen to attend. Then, one day, shortly before I graduated, I was talking to a friend in passing. "Stephanie," he said, "I don't think you'll like the environment you'll have at the University of Iowa. It's a big school. I think you'll get lost there". It was as if God was speaking directly to me through my friend. I got the message, but I was bewildered. I had already been accepted to my first-choice school, the college I had known I would attend since I was eight. But that night, with no other reason than that I was stepping out in faith, I followed my intuition, called U of I, and told them I would not be attending in the fall. Immediately afterward, I called the college that I had said I would never attend— the college, incidentally, where my mother and brother had both attended—and asked them if they would accept my application. A small private institution, Mid-America Nazarene University was about the size of my high school, and I had never before seen it as a place I wanted to be. But it is where I ended up. And it was where I was meant to be all along.

Our Sixth Sense: The Still, Small Voice of Intuition

Don't trust your intuition, empower it.

— Gabby Bernstein

Fiji is a string of islands in the South Pacific Ocean. A place on many people's bucket lists, it captures the definition of paradise. Picturesque bungalows on stilts are spread over the crystal clear aqua marine waters. Colorful clownfish, butterflyfish, and lion-fish dance through the water, entertaining snorkelers as they soak up the sun. For many this is a once in a lifetime vacation. The idea of Fiji I had in my mind was precisely this picture perfect landscape, and I was ready to experience the beauty that awaited.

When we landed in Fiji, however, it quickly became apparent that my actual experience would be different then what I had dreamed up in my mind. Joby had decided that we would have an *authentic* Fijian experience.

While Fiji has magnificent landscapes I found myself in a different place altogether. First Landing, a village on Fiji's main island, is so named because, according to local legend, the first Fijians arrived on its beach around 1500 BC. By the look of it, not much had changed since then. The township was rustic. Small homes with thatched roofs were sprinkled throughout the community and surrounded by lush greenery.

We were warned not to go in the local waters due to extreme pollution. I figured I could cope with that restriction for a few days. The community at First Landing graciously opened their homes to us; our host welcomed us with a traditional kava kava ceremony that is thousands of years old. Once you drink kava kava with a community, you are considered to be forever connected to the people and the land.

Harvested and ground up by hand, the finely ground, gray kava kava powder is placed in a cheesecloth-like mesh and submerged in water. An elder chants a prayer over the mixture as he massages through the water the sock full of ground kava kava. The water grows increasingly muddy-looking. The cloudy gray mixture is considered ready when it looks like a sink of dirty potato water.

Despite the deep cultural significance of the ceremony, thoughts crossed my mind like: "I wonder how recently that sock was washed. Has everyone washed their hands today?" And "Is that bottled water they're using, or should I be concerned about drinking the water?"

I sat cross-legged on the ground with the men in the community, preparing to join in communion with them. One small coconut shell cup is shared by everyone as the wooden bowl is passed from person to person, around the circle again and again, until the liquid is gone. Looking at the murky kava water, repeating words I did not understand, asking for translations of what was being spoken, and drinking cup after cup of the grayish concoction was surreal. As the liquid flowed down my throat, a sense of numbness washed over my face. My body gradually seemed to transition to another time and space, to an alternative state of being. I felt as though I was drifting through the clouds, light and disconnected.

Our kava kava ceremony.

Our hut was a small structure with a thatched roof and dirt floor; no electricity, bathroom, or door. The moment I stepped through the doorway, my intuition said, "Don't sleep in the bed." Our hosts had obviously worked to make our accommodations appealing and I was thankful for the effort. Yet, I could not shake my uneasy feeling. I voiced my concern to Joby, but he thought I was being silly.

I knew I wasn't going to sleep. It was so hot, and I kept thinking about the bugs and spiders I couldn't see that could be crawling all around—or what could be lurking on the other side of the doorway to the hut, which was wide open for anything to come scurrying in.

I did what any girl in my circumstance would do. I covered every square inch of my body with clothing. It was over 100 degrees outside but I was determined not to expose my skin to the possibility of creepy-crawly things. I put on my socks, jeans, and hooded sweatshirt. I sat all night with my knees drawn into my chest on the rickety metal chair in a corner of the hut. Joby insisted that I was overreacting and that I would regret not getting a good night's sleep with such a big day ahead of us. No matter what he said, I couldn't bring myself to lay on the bed. Joby, on the other hand, immediately stripped down to his boxers and flopped into bed, snuggling in for a restful evening. I was miserable, sweating profusely as I hovered in the corner.

At last, morning broke. As rays of sunlight penetrated the slits in the boards that comprised the walls of the hut, it became like a sauna. I jumped from my perch into the sunlight to stretch.

Joby rose. As he stretched his arms above his head, I gasped, catching my first glimpse of the red bites that consumed his entire body. He was literally covered in large red welts. Not yet realizing his own predicament, he instantly began to tell me I had overreacted the night before, that he had slept great and that I looked ridiculous huddled in the corner dressed for winter when I was in paradise. Then he began to itch. The look of panic on his face said it all before he blurted out, "My whole body itches!" I told him not to scratch, but he did so anyway. When mosquitoes and plenty of other bugs bite, they excrete a tiny amount of anesthetic that allows them to feed vampire-like, without being noticed; but they also leave the equivalent of some of their saliva, ultimately causing a histamine reaction that only gets worse when scratched. In fact, the scratching can cause not just swelling and a worse sensation of itching, it can lead to infection. I figured that whatever had bitten Joby couldn't be all that different.

Looking down at himself, Joby suddenly noticed the now quarter-sized bug bites covering his body. We began to suspect almost instantly that bedbugs were the culprits that had been feasting on him all night long. The itchy sensation increased. I was disgusted. Joby looked as if he had super big chickenpox covering his body. As he scratched, they were becoming brighter shades of red by the minute. Clearly, I wasn't so silly anymore. He was willing to listen to me as to next steps—leaving immediately so that all of our things could be sterilized, showering, and getting Joby some ointment to soothe his profusion of bedbug bites. We thanked our hosts, gave them some gifts, and were on our way. The immersion in local culture had been a memorable experience, but I was now ready for a different experience.

Prior to the stay in that hut, I'd had no idea what a bedbug even looked like, so I had to Google what I was seeing in order to be sure my instincts were correct. As it turned out, bedbugs look a lot like ticks and similarly suck blood from the hosts to whom they attach. These little creatures are nighttime ninjas that attack while you're sound asleep, wreaking havoc on your skin. You only know they've been there because you itch like you've just rolled in a field of poison ivy; the red, swelling, itchy bumps can plague the host for days to weeks. For Joby, it would take three weeks to heal.

We ended up at an upscale hotel to regroup. Once we had ourselves together, we decided to explore the rest of the main island. Lush green mountains roll over the island of Fiji. Along the ridge of a rocky mountain that rises up out of the forest, we could make out the head, body, and feet of a sleeping giant, known locally as the man on the mountain. Local legend says that the giant will one day awake, and it's not hard to see how such a possibility might be believed.

Driving to the base of the mountain, we took a dip in the mud baths. It's not actually a bath in the way most people in Western culture would understand it at all; quiet the contrary, one actually ends up getting very dirty during a soak. We jumped in without hesitation when we were told that the mud in these pits could heal the body. It seemed the perfect thing to soothe Joby's skin after his run-in with those pesky bedbugs.

On the way back to the hotel, we saw two girls waiting for a bus on an almost deserted road in the middle of the jungle. Joby decided we should pick them up. But I had the intuitive feeling that we shouldn't. Joby won out. The girls were nice, both nurses visiting from England. They were staying at a hostel twenty minutes in the opposite direction from where we were headed, and needed a ride back to their accommodations. About a mile from their hostel, Joby was making a left hand turn when we were sideswiped by an on-coming car that failed to stop. The gentleman driving the other car got out. Obviously very upset, he was yelling at us. He insisted on calling the police to assess the scene. We agreed it was probably the best course of action. None of us had a phone, and we didn't know what else to do at that point.

Two police cars arrived, and the officers immediately began to question us. We were dumbfounded. Our car, after all, was the one that had been hit! As the dialogue unfolded, however, it became clear that the two policemen were the brother and cousin of the man who had hit us. It wasn't looking good for us.

The officers asked who had been driving. Joby raised his hand. The officers declared they were going to take him into custody until he paid a fine. Things were getting worse by the minute. We asked what the charges were, why the other driver wasn't being held responsible and what was really going on. I took a bunch of pictures of the accident which, on second glance, didn't look like that big of a deal—a few scratches, a small dent, definitely not a need for the drama that was transpiring. Yet, there wasn't anything I could do at that point but follow the police, who now had Joby in their custody.

When we arrived at the police station, the other driver was nowhere to be found. He had been completely free to go about his day. His uniformed cousin explained to me that in Fiji the law was different than in America; in order for Joby to be released, we would have to pay he and his colleague $600 USD in cash.

The accident was not our fault, but we were in a predicament. It was a Friday night. We could pay the $600 the two officers were demanding, or Joby would sit in jail for the weekend—actually, until we could find someone to represent us and figure out the scam they were evidently running to rip off tourists. Having Joby locked up in jail for the weekend was not acceptable to us. Against our will, we complied with the demand for cash.

The corrupt policemen had to walk us to two different ATMs, as we had placed a cash withdrawal limit on our respective credit cards. Once they had the money in hand the two men finally let us go. While we were relieved, we felt so violated.

That 48-hour period was a lesson in the power of intuition. In each instance that I had listened to my instincts—my inner guide—I had benefitted. In each instance I'd ignored the nudging of my instincts—or allowed them to be ignored by others—a tough lesson had been delivered, one that could have been avoided. Moving forward, I determined, I would pay attention to my inner guide. Living an intuitive life is the easy answer to the challenges we face. It is, in fact, the result of a properly functioning mind-heart connection.

We all tend to be aware of our 5 physical senses: touch, taste, sight, hearing, and smell. These senses comprise our reality. Removed from these physical sensations, we have what many would call a sixth sense, though some do not pay as much attention to its presence in our day-to-day lives as the other five.

Our brain is a great interpreter of information. It processes life via the data it receives from our five senses; but it typically does not utilize our most powerful sense, the sixth sense or what is often referred to as our intuition. Intuition has been vastly undervalued, largely because it has not been properly understood. So, before we move on, we should take a closer look at the concept of intuition, what it is, and what factors enable a person to rely on their intuition.

Our five senses keep us grounded in our body. They protect us and provide feedback from our environment. Intuition furthers the information that our five senses yield by aligning *with* them. Strictly speaking, then, intuition is not a physical sensation as the other five senses are. Rather, it is a leveraging of the existing five senses to asses a situation quickly. In many cases, then, intuition is simply the ability to read one's environment and other people more efficiently—to gather and synthesize in a split second subtle data points that others might overlook. An intuitive person, for instance, might pick up on a hint of sweat on a person's upper lip, a minor slip of the tongue, and a quick dart of someone's eyes to know that they're nervous about something or not being completely honest. That information, in turn, allows better decision-making about what's happening in the situation and whether to trust someone, though others might miss such cues altogether. This ability to read the environment more deeply brings us into heart-centered living, where the brain and the heart work together to guide our understanding and choices. As a result, leveraging our intuition also tends to bring a sense of peace.

The good news is that, with time and practice, anyone can begin to leverage the highly refined skill of deeply read environmental cues.

When we hone intuition, it can develop even deeper roots and meaning in our life. Cultivating our intuition overrides our mind, allowing us to see things as they really are, not simply as our mind imagines or wishes them to be. Intuition allows us to interpret data, pulling wisdom from our surroundings and promptly utilizing it in our daily life.

We are intelligently designed. Within each and every one of us is an innate wisdom, an internal navigation system that consistently guides us. Some call it a gut feeling, some call it intuition; whatever you call it, listen when it speaks. Listening expedites the journey to achieving the purpose we were placed here to accomplish. There is only one of you in all of time. The world is waiting for your expression and impact.

Everyone is intuitive, for intuition is the language of the soul. However, because our intuition speaks softly, it is often drowned out by the loud, noisy voice of the ego. The ego, remember is all about the past and the future; if we listen to it, it will rob us of the now and our joy. When our intuition speaks, we know we're in the present moment. That's important, because life is an inner journey that makes sense in the present. Intuition leverages the experiences of the past to help us read current and future environmental cues more accurately. We learn as we harness the assistance that intuition offers in the present. To open ourselves and hear our intuition more clearly, we must find a way to quiet ourselves and remain in the present moment, keeping our mind free from the clutter of aimless thoughts that continually bombard our consciousness. The quieted mind is much better able to focus and more receptive to the messages either available in the environment or spoken by others. In being open and trusting our intuition, we will begin to hear when it speaks.

We cannot turn off our connection to intuition just as we cannot disconnect ourselves from our Creator. We *can*, however, suppress intuition by not listening, just as we can push out the wisdom that God offers in our lives by denying our belief.

In the not so distant past, the human species struggled daily against environmental elements in order to survive. We literally depended upon our built-in fight-or-flight mechanism to protect ourselves against the harsh realities life threw at us moment by moment.

Fight-or-flight relies on the physiological responses of our five senses. When our body is pushed into that mode, our awareness heightens, our respiratory rate increases, and adrenaline floods the body. Understandably, then, prolonged fight-or-flight stresses the body to exhaustion. In fact, if our bodies can't properly metabolize all of the hormones in which prolonged fight-or-flight can result, a host of health disorders and diseases can result, including adrenal fatigue, inflammation, and high blood pressure among them. Living in such a state was never what the Creator intended for us, though it remains helpful in short bursts to preserve life. It has a place, and it's there when we do need it. But in modern society, we don't generally have to think about sabertooth tigers chasing us in the bush or the raw basics of survival.

Where fight-or-flight is fear-based and reactionary, intuition is gentle guidance, directing us from a place of knowing. It doesn't spark the physiological response that fight-or-flight does. Rather, where fight-or-flight causes us to run away from a negative circumstance, intuition aligns us to the moment from a place of peacefulness, empowering us to take the right action.

Yet, despite our modern circumstances, often we fall into the trap of seeing life a bit like cavemen; we tend to view things as one mini-emergency after another. We function in a state of overreaction. Society loves to push fear upon us. The media, for example, hypes fear of sickness and disease, sensationalizes stories in a way that leads us to believe that everyone is the enemy, and makes us feel that we must always be watching our back. These scare tactics put our mind in a constant state of fight-or-flight. To effectively manage this response in society today, it thus becomes even more important that we figure out how properly to assess the signals of danger and the potential threat we feel. Is the feedback we're receiving accurate? Are we in immediate danger? Are we overreacting?

Acknowledging our intuitiveness in past circumstances allows us to be more open to seeing and listing to our intuition moving forward. Think of a time when you clearly heard your intuition. Maybe you listened to it, maybe not. You'll know right away if it was a time you should have listened, because you'll hear yourself thinking or saying, "I knew something was off," or, "I knew I should have [fill in the blank]." Take note of each of these experiences. When we recount the times we heard our intuition speaking to us, many of the red flags that we ignored come into sharper focus.

How about when you step into a new situation or meet people, ask yourself a couple of questions. How does the encounter feel? Does it feel negative? Do you experience uncomfortable resistance, or does it feel good and comfortable? When you pause for a moment, quieting your mind and opening your awareness, what naturally pops into your mind? Don't overthink it. Just note what is being spoken within. Ask yourself why it feels the way it does.

We have all met people and instantly felt the positive or negative vibe they were giving off. Due to this initial encounter, we decided this was someone we wanted to steer clear of or maybe they were someone we were wildly drawn to. There are instances in life where our mind says, "This is the right direction," and it may even make logical sense; but it doesn't resonate in your heart center. This is exactly the sort of circumstance in which intuition will show us the true direction.

For instance: imagine that a business deal you have been searching for crosses your path. It looks perfect on paper. Yet, your intuition for some reason says, "Don't do it." Be mindful of this nudge and follow where it is leading. Accept the no; your intuition is speaking up on your behalf. Then ask yourself an additional question or two. Not, "Should I do this deal with this person?" That question only challenges your inner voice. Instead, investigate the answer that your inner voice is expressing and why it is coming into conflict with what your logical mind is telling you. Some good questions to ask, for example, include: "Am I inclined to take this path due to ego or fear? Does this business venture facilitate my spiritual growth and healing? Is it what I am intended to do? Will it positively impact my life, the lives of others, or the world?" All of these considerations peel back layers of self-preservation.

After taking all considerations to heart, return to the questions immediately at hand: "Is this the right direction? Is it true? How does it feel?" Gravitating away from what feels heavy and toward what feels light and right. When we ask and are open to the answer, it will be revealed in perfect time. Intuition will answer.

Worried about what happens if you go against your intuition and make a mistake? We've all done it plenty of times in our lives. Fear not! The universe has an amazing way of working itself out. If you get off track, you can instantly head back onto the right track. The key is quick realignment. Ask for guidance, be open to a different path, and let go of the attachment to how you or others around you think things should be. Listening expedites the journey to achieving the purpose we were placed here to accomplish. There is only one of you in all of time and the world is waiting for your expression and impact. Let us be a light to the world by living through the light within us.

Without going too deep into the law of vibration within Quantum Physics, we know that atoms resonate or vibrate at different frequencies or in particular patterns. Every object in the world around us is essentially composed of energy moving at diverse speeds. Think about it like this: our senses are vibration translators. Our eyes translate vibration to create the colors we see. Our ears interpret frequencies into the sounds we hear. The lightest touch creates a vibration in our body that awakens our nerves. We constantly project and receive environmental and emotional energy with the world around us. For example, I've found that living in gratitude and maintaining a thankful attitude allows me to function—vibrate—in a way that increases my sense of peace and happiness. At the same time, my vibrations become a beacon for others, encouraging them along a similar path. It becomes important, then, to protect our healthy energy, or vibration. In each situation, take note of how you feel. Similarly, connecting to situations or other people negatively will always compromise both your state of mind and any outcomes. For instance, instead of matching the negative emotions others may be conveying, adopt an attitude of openness. From there, it becomes possible to recognize another's point of view without taking it on. This approach also allows us to be of greater service to those around us. The truth is, we are unable to help other people by taking on their stuff as our own. They have experiences and lessons of their own that they need to work through, just as we do. It's actually imperative, then, that we allow everyone their own experiences and the blessings of growth that come with them. In fact, even by feeling sorry for them, trying to fix them, or attempting to resolve their situation for them, we're actually doing two detrimental things. First, we're judging them and the path they're on. Second, by engaging in such judgement and the perception that we're better than them, we're actually disempowering the other person and robbing them of important opportunities to create their own new reality. When we empower others to grow, we empower ourselves and grow, too. How is that possible, I hear you wondering.

The cost to us of allowing our emotional energy to be compromised is, in fact, quite high. In and through openness—and compassion with healthy boundaries—we recognize that growth and evolution is occurring in others. We can better maintain not only a space of love for them, empowering them to heal, but also protect and nurture our own positive state of mind. What I'm identifying, here, is the need to set healthy boundaries on how you engage with the relationship—boundaries that will facilitate the relationship while always supporting you. That's what this book is all about—stepping outside of our comfort zones to create new experiences that bring about growth and healing.

Caterpillars Were Meant To Fly

If you wish to understand the Universe, think
of energy, frequency and vibration.

— Nikola Tesla

A caterpillar is born from an egg and all it knows is that it is a caterpillar. The caterpillar lives its life in the reality that it is a caterpillar. Each day it interacts with its environment, crawling around plants, eating leaves and letting the sun shine on its back. One day its instinct tells it to make a cocoon. Does the caterpillar realize that this act is a formatted death for the life that it's known? I'm not sure.

In the cocoon the caterpillar digests itself. It breaks down what no longer serves it so that it can develop into that which it is truly meant to be: a beautiful butterfly. When the caterpillar emerges from the cocoon, its reality will be dramatically altered. The caterpillar struggles to get free of the cocoon, to remove itself from the old way of being. During the process of emergence, the butterfly pushes fluids though its body that inflate its wings properly. If the caterpillar does not struggle through the process, in fact, it can never truly become a butterfly. If you take the butterfly from the cocoon prematurely, for instance, it will likely be crippled and never able to fly on its own. Once this difficult process has taken place, however, the butterfly no longer crawls around the garden plants or eats leaves. The former caterpillar now soars around the garden with gossamer wings and drinks the nectar of flowers.

As human beings we must also journey through a metamorphosis. When we are born, we are in many ways a clean slate to the world. We receive feedback as to how to act and what our lives should be. When we're ready, we gravitate towards change. We go within. We digest what we've learned and begin to unlearn and discard that which no longer serves us. We develop a whole new outlook of who we are and what we are here to do. Remarkably, we find our new reality by shedding and letting go of the known—the familiar. "It's the end of the world," said the caterpillar. "It's the beginning of the world," said the butterfly. It's all in how we look at things. In our walk with God, we go through similar stages of death and rebirth.

As we look at the world around us, its constant changing and the massive shifts that happen in culture and society it can be daunting. But why take on the weight of the changing world? It's an impossible task. Instead doesn't it make more sense to change ourselves and let the world follow? This is actually the way things can and do work. But it won't if we're not willing to give up that which we currently are to become that which we are meant to be.

The world is not what it appears to be. There are vibrational energies flowing through the ether around us every day, but the frequency to which we're tuned changes on a moment by moment basis. I am a firm believer in meditation and the ability we have to recharge the body when we choose to get still and reflect on what we're feeding the spirit. Meditation helps us clear the chatter in our mind. When we focus, we're choosing to listen to the whispers of God. The soul seeks to align with the wisdom of our Creator and to be healed. Meditation turns down the noise, making it easier for us to hear

God talking to us—to reconnect with the Creator and consider the wisdom being offered to us.

In a large sense, whatever receives our energy and emotion becomes our reality. We all put up protective barriers to create a sense of security from the chaos of the world. Meditation opens the door to divine wisdom. The security and freedom we are searching for comes from God, the one who created us, died for us, set us free, and lives within us. In every circumstance we strive to be the best version of ourselves, to express our infinite potential and most of all live as God has commanded. Meditation helps bring us back to our center, restore balance, and bring us increasingly in tune with the spirit.

I vividly remember a specific night that I prayed for Gods guidance in my life. I meditated, said my prayers, and went to bed. As I drifted to sleep, my conscious mind gave way to my subconscious mind. In these sleeping hours I saw a vision of a beautiful bright white light. It was warm and powerful, like a bear hug from someone you love, though it lasted only as long as it would take you to snap your fingers. Just before I awoke, I heard a clear message, "Follow me, and you will be shown the truth." With a jolt I awoke and sat straight up in bed. I had received the message. I could feel the excitement in every cell as my body react to what I had just experienced.

I sat there for a couple moments focusing on my breath, all of my senses on high alert. In fact, the title and concepts for this book are not my own; I honed them from that experience and the message I was instantly given to share. My waking mind was bewildered, How could any of this be real? Was it true?

Disbelieving of what just occurred, I did a quick Google search. Surely the title and domain "Food Of The Spirit" was taken. Nope. That was all the confirmation I needed to move forward. I got up out of bed to write down concepts, questions, and thoughts that flooded my mind. For hours I wrote without ceasing. That night was the birth of the book you now hold in your hands.

The vision I experienced was burned into my mind; it was not a typical dream, fleeting in the moments after we wake. If I close my eyes now I can relive it. In fact, looking back on my life, I will always see this moment as a key turning point.

Aside from yielding the vision for this book, this experience also gave me something else that was deeply important. It became clear to me that, while we're often told that knowledge is power, it is the application of knowledge that truly transforms our lives. When we are able to quiet our own ego, which distracts and pulls us away from God, we are able to delve far more deeply into our journey. We can do—and *achieve*—things that would not be possible if we were not listening to the Creator.

By being open to the beautiful masterpiece that the Creator has outlined for our lives, together with him we can co-create a vibrantly colored masterpiece. So many wonderful things are in store for us. When we look at the world through the word of God, we see the truth. Christ has empowered you to do miracles in his name as He works through you.

When we look at the world through this lens it transforms our perspective. We don't give up on the world or the people who occupy it; rather, the way we act and interact changes as God works through us. Our trust should not be in the world but in our Creator. In shifting our perspective away from worldly living, the things of this world lose their ability to hurt or affect us.

While that's a simply stated goal, it's not as easy as it may sound. How well I know! Part of the problem is that illusions surround us in our linear, earthly lives. For instance, the chair on which you're sitting seems solid. Yet, in reality, it's constructed of individual molecules that are simply a form of energy. As discussed earlier in the book, we often convince ourselves we're victims in a situation. That's a common illusion into which we can fall. Yet, reality demonstrates that there is never any power or benefit in looking at things from that perspective.

However difficult it may sometimes be, you always have the ability—the choice—to make your experience positive or negative. You have the ability to change the way you look at things. Through your perspective, create the experience that will enable you to grow, thrive, understand, achieve, and so much more.

Look at each moment as a process of Creation. Normalcy in its current state may just be insanity. We have the ability as transformed individuals to shift the state of normal to a new paradigm, like the caterpillar does when it transforms and takes wing.

Use The "F" Word Often

We do not heal the past by dwelling there; we
heal the past by living fully in the present.

— Marianne Williamson

Each thought we think has an energy associated with it. Our thoughts translate into emotion and physical experience. We all have emotional baggage that we have worked through or are still working through. In fact, as human beings, we have a strong sense of self-preservation. We build and maintain walls in our mind so that we don't have to face the emotional monsters we've created. But when we push the monsters into the closet, we allow them to fester in our lives, creating much bigger problems than if we had begun dealing with them the moment they raised their ugly heads.

We are all different. Fear, anger, guilt, shame—or whatever else is undermining our ability to thrive as God has intended—could be lifelong problems for one person but non-issues for another. We learn some lessons faster than others, and no two people heal or grow at the same pace. If we think of the issues we face in life as though they are an onion, we can begin to grasp this concept. An onion has many layers. As we peel back each layer, we get closer to the core. When we examine the issues in our lives, they always have a core. The more we peel back the layers, the more progress we make toward reaching and addressing the core issue that will bring about healing. As we deal with those issues accordingly, they subside. How does this happen? As we peel back the layers, we make new discoveries about ourselves, our wounds, and our strengths. All of these insights provide spiritual food for us to heal and grow. When we deal with issues only at a surface level, however, they will inevitably spring up in the future because we never pushed through to the core.

You are safe to acknowledge negative feelings along with the sweeter ones in life. But when we experience hurt and choose not to release it, it can turn into resentment. Resentment is a debilitating energy and hinders our spiritual growth. By contrast, forgiveness feeds the spirit, as it has the means to instantly dispel negative energy. Saying, "I forgive but I'll never forget," is actually tragic, because it's not true forgiveness. In fact, in the moment they are thought or spoken, resentment is actually being cultivated. Resentment does not spring forth from the conduct of another; it is present due to our unwillingness to end the altercation and replace it with forgiveness. In choosing to release the hurt, we find peace.

Are you harboring a past hurt? Are you willing to allow that hurt the power to continue impacting you negatively? People and circumstances in our lives are either a blessing or a lesson. The fact we tend to miss is that all lessons, once learned, *become* blessings.

Embracing the lessons our experiences hold is what unlocks them, enabling us to experience the blessings. The challenge, of course, is that lessons frequently involve some measure of pain. Often that pain comes via other people. When people hurt us, forgiveness will ultimately have to come into play if we're going to avoid being stymied or stunted. Moreover, forgiveness is, in a large sense, a spiritual muscle that grows stronger when we exercise it. The more quickly we learn to deal with issues, the more emotional nimbleness and courage we will have the next time we are faced with the choice of either suppressing the emotions and undermining ourselves or working through the emotion, exercising forgiveness, and stretching into more positive experiences. Choose kindness over being right and do it for yourself. Let's not get confused on this important point. Being kind does not mean you make yourself a doormat to be walked over. Having healthy boundaries is vital and we can act in kindness while maintaining boundaries that serve us.

When we are upset and holding onto inner turmoil, we're not living our best life. What we're experiencing can stand alone; there's no reason to attach blame or to identify with anything negative. Just because another wants to place blame, does not mean you have to take on that blame. The most responsible thing we can do is to rectify the situation. We do that through our reaction, by politely refusing either to become a scapegoat or to place blame. When we release the need to identify with how others think or feel about us it is freeing. No one can control us or dictate to us how we should feel about ourselves. We have the authority to reject these projections and refuse consent to their effect in our life. Releasing the need to blame others or yourself for a perceived wrong creates the ability to focus on ourselves and take responsibility for how we choose to respond. We alone have the power to change our perception of the situation. Other people only acquire that power when we give it to them. In the moment that we make up our mind to forgive, the situation instantly changes. When we accept responsibility for the role we play, we affirm our power to learn from and change it.

Forgiveness is the foundation to fully loving ourselves and others. While sometimes we've held something against a person wrongly, and they actually deserve our forgiveness, most of the time we're in a position of having to forgive and let go when the person who's wronged us hasn't even asked for our forgiveness. They may not know or even care about the harm they've done. This reality raises a crucial point: Forgiveness of others is more often than not a gift we give to ourselves. Forgiveness isn't so much about the other person being deserving as it is about our need for peace. When we do not forgive, we stunt our own growth, which actually harms only us. Getting caught up in your head over who is right or wrong is a dangerous sand trap. As hard as it may be, the best thing you can do for yourself is let it go. It all comes down to healing. Forgiveness frees us.

Forgiveness also allows us to experience relationship with God in a way we can't when we're holding on to pain and hurt. Again, it's not about what someone else did or didn't do, it's the effect we allow it to have on us. What we choose as our focus expands. Perpetuating the circumstances of other people's problems, pain, and projections, then, is not a great place to be. The miracle you experience through forgiveness is a shift from fear to love. That powerful shift to love within us can foster miracles. Not only is it possible of spurring a similar awakening of love in the person that has hurt us, but it can bring about the end of turmoil both within that person and with them interpersonally.

The unresolved issues we suppress can create stress in our lives and stress can create symptoms in the body that are harmful to our well-being. As well as emotional distress, symptoms could include: physical tension, anxiety attacks, depression, sleep problems, and digestive and heart issues. The cumulative effects on our body could lead to disease or we can choose to release the negative energy and manifest healing in our lives.

When we find it hard to forgive, it is because we are not living in the present moment. We are instead allowing the past to steal our joy. Whether we want to go through the situation or not, it is present in our lives for our development. Forgiveness is an act of love—an active process that brings us closer to God.

Forgiveness has multiple effects that ripple outward. In point of fact, as we've already discussed, only changing ourselves is likely to result in other people choosing to change. Similarly, only changing how we *respond* to the world can achieve change *in* the world.

Nourishing ourselves with the food of the spirit requires daily forgiveness of ourselves and others. Is there something in your life for which you need forgiveness? Someone else you need to forgive? Whoever or whatever needs to be released and forgiven at this moment, take a second to pray about it. Call the person weighing on your heart, write them a letter, or simply let the matter go. Whatever you do, do it now.

There are steps we take in actively forgiving ourselves and others. When asking for forgiveness, remember these steps:

1) I'm sorry
2) I was wrong.
3) I'll try not to do it again.
4) What can I do to make things right?
5) Would you please forgive me?

Seeking forgiveness in earnest from another might sound something like this: "[Insert person's name], I am sorry for hurting your feelings. It was wrong of me to [state the grievance]. I will try not to do it again. What can I do to make things right? Will you please forgive me?"

If the person or situation is not conducive to this conversation, forgiveness can still occur. We have the ability to forgive even when the person that hurt us is not sorry. Decide that from this point on your response will be to forgive others and yourself at *every* opportunity. In taking this outlook, we can enter each situation with open arms and avoid complete upset. It may not always be easy—and it may take time—but do it anyway. It is what your soul needs to be free and at peace. As forgiveness becomes your focus, in fact, your peace will be preserved.

We do not go through life unscathed. In this life, there will be wounds along the way, and situations will always arise that we do not like or with which we do not agree. But what if, through our wounds, we find a way to let in light that not only binds and heals our wounds but brings a new and valuable perspective? The scar alone will remain as a testament of how strong we were. We always have control over our responses. In the final analysis, it matters not whether we agree or disagree with, like or dislike something. What *does* matter is the state of our mind and spirit. If our peace is being disturbed, forgiveness is always the answer. When we choose to hold the victim mentality, we are not punishing the other person; we are directly hurting ourselves.

This wisdom is central to the Christian spiritual tradition. Jesus tells us in Mark 11:25:

> And whenever you stand praying, forgive, if you have anything against anyone, so that your Father also who is in heaven may forgive you your trespasses.
>
> — English Standard Version (ESV)

In offering forgiveness, we give and receive peace. The giving and receiving is, in a large sense, one in the same. We forgive because, God first loved and forgave us.[4] We cannot extend that which we have not already received and accepted personally. The requirement that we extend the forgiveness that we have already received is not some arbitrary demand on God's part. He simply knows it is to our benefit. In giving forgiveness and peace, we experience forgiveness

---

[4] I John 4:19

and peace. Similarly, when we apologize we release the error in our way and allow the love that is our truth to shine. Dissolving the error clears room for something better, including a new personal program that frees us. Recognizing the conflict allows us to discern how we are assigning value, determine whether that assignment may be in error, and redirect if necessary in order to shift to a state of reconciliation.

God has placed assignments on our lives. We were created with unique talents and burdens that He uses to advance the kingdom here on earth. Our calling, as II Timothy 1:9 explains, begins with the one who calls us: "not according to our world, but according to His own purpose and grace which was given to us in Christ Jesus before time began." Getting where we're meant to go is less about pushing—which involves our own efforts—and more about aligning with our Creator and the beneficial principles he established. Forgiveness is one thing we can do to align with God and the mission He has given us in this world. Forgiveness, in fact, affords us the opportunity to align not only to the spiritual source that supports us but also to the truth concerning who we are and need to be.

Love Is The Answer, No Matter The Question

When it's time for souls to meet, there's nothing on earth that can prevent them from meeting, no matter where each may be located.

— Jaime Lichauco

There was a time that I questioned if I would ever meet my "soulmate." What is a soulmate, anyway? I was beginning to think it was a term that people used to convince themselves that the person they were with was their only possible match in a world of seven billion people; a way of comforting themselves that they hadn't settled.

All of my married friends would try to comfort me that *"the one"* was out there. In my reality as a single person, there were plenty of guys I thought could be a great match for me, and with whom I imagined I could be happy building a life. Each one of those guys was smart, funny, and handsome. What was there not to like or find promising? For one reason or another, however, they didn't work out, and over time I had come to the realization that being single wasn't all that bad. I could focus on being the best possible me without any distractions. It's often been said that one finds love most easily when one isn't looking for it. Perhaps that's just another way of saying that love begins with an acceptance of what is.

Meeting Joby was an unexpected encounter. When he walked into my office for the first time, I couldn't have known how dramatically my life would change—that it would be flipped upside down, with every day holding wildly unexpected adventures and pushing me to the limit. Nor could I have believed that I would be more in love with Joby after years together than on the day I said, "I do." Yet, something deep down inside me *did* tell me that he was the one with whom I would spend the rest of my life. But I'm getting ahead of myself...

I was working in a dental office when, one day, the dentist for whom I worked came in and told me he'd heard an ad on a local Christian radio station and that he wanted to consult with Joby on a business opportunity. He handed me a piece of paper with Joby's number on it, then went about his day.

I was slightly bewildered, since I had not heard the ad. I wasn't sure what Joby did for work, and with such little insight I had no idea how to approach getting him in for a visit. Nevertheless, I picked up the phone and dialed. An answering machine picked up. The recording was quite odd: "Aloha, you've reached Joby Weeks. My office hours are Mondays from 12 to 12:08. If you have reached me outside of these hours, please leave a message."

"Eight minutes of office hours? On Mondays only? That couldn't be possible. Either this guy is really cocky, a joker, or he doesn't know that half of his message is missing," I thought to myself. I left a message with our office number but received no call back.

A few days later I tried again. To be fair, my second call was not within his aforementioned office hours. I called him in the afternoon, mid-week, meaning four more days off before his next 8-minute shift. So perhaps I shouldn't have been surprise by his lack of response. He had, however, taken the time to change his message:

"Aloha, this is Joby Weeks. I am out of the country traveling through the Caribbean, then Mexico. If this is urgent, please reach me on my satellite phone."

"Who *is* this guy?" I wondered to myself. Flabbergasted, I left another professional message and went about my day.

As a few weeks rolled by with no call back from this mysterious character, the dentist began questioning me as to why he still did not have an appointment with Mr. Weeks on the books. All I could tell him was, "This guy doesn't return calls, and he obviously isn't worried about scheduling any appointments procured from his radio ad."

Desperate times call for desperate measures. I tried a third time. I knew he must have picked up my earlier messages, because the recording on the answering machine had changed yet again: "Aloha, this is Joby Weeks. I will be traveling through Europe and Australia. I'll call you when I get back. Leave a message."

This time, I tried a new tactic: "Aloha, Joby. This is Stephanie. I hope you know I expect to go on one of these trips with you one day. Call me." I left my phone number.

As I hung up the phone I felt a rush of heat flow over my body. "How unprofessional," I chided myself. "I'm probably going to lose my job over this."

But it worked. Joby called me back that afternoon. He was very easy to chat with, and we giggled about the message I'd left. When he'd heard it, he thought I must be a girl he'd met somewhere along the way and promised to take on a trip. I thought to myself "Hey, whatever gets you in the office for lunch with the boss."

It was difficult to find a time that worked with Joby's hectic travel schedule, but we finally found a date a few weeks out. I got him on the books for a cleaning, as a new patient, with a lunch meeting with the doctor right after. I had occasion to talk with him on the phone at least twice more before the scheduled appointment. Each time, I enjoyed the banter so much that I began to think to myself, "If this guy turns out to be attractive, I'm in really big trouble."

It was the day of Mr. Weeks' appointment. I confess that I made sure to wear something extra cute to work. Arriving at the office early, as usual, I received a call from Joby. He wanted to cancel his appointment for that day. I refused to let him off early. I had put too much effort into getting him on the schedule. I told him that, if he would like to cancel, I would have to charge his account $50 for not giving us a required 24-hour notice. I would likely never have been able to collect the fee, but I hoped that my words would drive home the importance of the meeting. There was a long pause on the other end of the phone. Joby acquiesced, agreeing to make his scheduled appointment time.

A few hours later, the door to the office opened. In walked Joby. Prior to this encounter, had anyone asked me if I believed in love at first sight, I would have given them a flat no. But it's true that when you know, you truly can know. The feeling hit me like a 10-ton truck. "Game over." I silently thought.

My heart fluttering, I handed Joby his paperwork to fill out while I tried not to act nervous. After his dental appointment, he and the doctor headed off to lunch. Luckily, Joby hadn't been to the dentist for a number of years and needed some additional visits to complete some needed care. If I could keep him to his appointment schedule, I would see him again.

When Joby arrived for his second appointment, I led him back to the chair. I sat down next to him, with instruments in hand, and we struggled to make small talk. I noted that he was wearing hiking shoes. At the time, I was hiking three days a week, so I asked where he liked to go. I got a blank stare. Did I have gnarly breath, or did he just not want to chat? I let it go and went about my work.

Joby's third and final appointment saw him all fixed up and out the door. But there was no engaging conversation between us—no evidence of the connection of which I'd been so sure the first day he'd entered the office. I was bewildered, wondering if I'd been wrong about everything. Had our conversation just been politeness on his part? Was there nothing there at all? I did my best to brush the whole thing off.

A few days later, the office phone rang. Joby was on the other end, asking if I would like to go to a basketball game when he got back from his next trip. Adopting an air of pleasant nonchalance, I said that sounded fun, and I agreed. We set a time. As I put down the phone, the nonchalance fell away entirely. I did the happy dance any girl does when she gets exciting news.

Weeks went by. Date night finally arrived. The evening remains one of my favorite early lessons in learning to go with the flow.

I drove to Joby's house after work. Greeting me at the door, he offered to show me his place. It was an amazing spot for a guy in his mid-20s to live—right on a water ski lake. It fueled my curiosity about what this guy did for a living to be able to afford such a great arrangement so quickly in life.

At the top of some stairs, we came to the living area, where an interesting surprise awaited me: five of Joby's best guy friends, all just hanging out. Wow, here was something new for a first date.

I adapted quickly. The seven of us hung out chatting for a while, until suddenly Joby shouted out, "Hey guys, it's time to go. Who is riding with who?" It was now a group date—me and six guys, another situation I'd never encountered before. It was my second need to adapt that evening. It wouldn't be the last.

When we arrived at the convention center, the parking lot only had about twenty cars in it, I was a little bewildered but I followed Joby inside. There was no basketball game. Instead, Joby had brought me to the Johnny Walker Whisky Tour. Another curious twist to the evening. The seven of us were ushered into a seating area where we were to drink samples of Whisky and learn the history of the brand. I didn't drink. Thinking on my feet again, I passed every glass to Joby. He was thrilled and went about enjoying the samples I had been poured. When the presentation was over, I drove him home.

Deciding to hit up some clubs after the whiskey tour, Joby's friends headed out for the night, leaving the two of us some time alone to chat.

At some point in our conversation, Joby proposed a wager: "Every time I tell you something you don't know, you have to give me a kiss."

"Pretty forward," I thought to myself. But, surprising even myself, I agreed to the terms. It had already been an interesting night. Usual responses seemed somehow out of place.

Joby began to ask me questions, the first of which was: "Do you know the definition of a dollar?" He gave me a hint. "It is not four quarters, ten dimes or one hundred pennies."

I thought for a minute before giving what turned out to be a couple of wrong answers. "Tell me the answer," I finally insisted.

"You do realize that means I get a kiss?" was his response. I was well aware. I smiled on the inside. It was a win-win situation.

Joby explained that a dollar is a formal guarantee of its value in gold. He elaborated, telling me about the gold standard and its history. In fact, he just kept talking, which was a far cry from the taciturn guy that had sat in my dental chair just a few weeks before. I waited for him to take a breath and give me a kiss. But the man just kept talking. Finally, he leaned in to claim his reward. When he kissed me, his lips were soft and light like a cool breeze fluttering over your face. It made the hair on the back of my neck stand up—in a good way.

Almost as soon as the kiss was done, he went back to reeling out facts. Finally, the hour growing late, I told him it was time for me to go home. But before I left, he asked if I might want to go to Breckenridge to ski the following Saturday. Of course I did, I spent my weekends skiing anyway. How a person plays actually reveals a lot about them, so this would be the perfect opportunity to get to know Joby better.

The following weekend, skiing was indeed in store. But first, we met for dinner—another group date, this time including more friends and Joby's parents at a crazy little Mexican joint that was much more about the entertainment than the food. Going with the flow once again, I had a marvelous time. We all did, in fact.

Together, we headed off with a couple of Joby's friends to the mountains of Breckenridge after dinner.

The next morning we hit the slopes. Wow, were these people good! Luckily I could keep up and enjoyed skiing straight down the face as quickly as possible. Joby didn't say so, but I'm pretty sure he was impressed that I could keep up with all the tests he was clearly throwing my way on the slopes and elsewhere.

The day was going fabulously, and it was gorgeous weather—sunny and pretty warm. The mountain conditions were also quite good, so we went hard on the slopes all day. Everything was perfect, in fact—until I almost died.

Skiing down the mountain, I had to swerve when a guy suddenly popped out of the woods and right into my path. In attempting to avoid him, I hit a patch of ice and went flying between two trees, about three feet apart, with a huge boulder in the middle.

When I awoke, other skiers were huddled over me, talking in not so hushed tones about how they had expected to come over and find me dead. One of my skis was propped up against the side of a tree, the other lay half-buried in the snow. Miraculously, I had been thrown over the boulder between the trees and come out of the incident without a single broken bone or scratch. I got up, brushed myself off, and put my skis back on so I could head back to the hotel. God had had his hand of mercy on me that day, as He does every day—a fact for which I praise him.

From that day forward, Joby and I were almost inseparable. I would work during the day, then drive forty minutes to his house in the evening to see him before heading home. We'd hang out on the weekends, too. If we were apart, it was only for a day or two.

It was during this early period of our relationship, however, that Joby's roommates clued me in: Joby, they explained, was considered an international playboy, and I was not the only girl he was seeing. My experience began to bear out the truth of what they were telling me. A couple of weeks in, for instance, a girl came into town to see Joby, a trip that he'd somehow forgotten had been planned months in advance. On Valentine's Day, I arrived at his house to find that he was at dinner with another girl. When I was working, he sometimes took other women out snowboarding. Questions about whether I wanted to move forward with the relationship understandably began to figure large in my mind.

The first company event I attended with Joby was a nightmare. More than one woman I'd never met marched up to me to tell me, "Back off. He's mine." I also had numerous people telling me to turn and run because Joby would only break my heart. I didn't just feel attacked and hurt in those moments, I felt conflicted "Was I right about Joby being 'the one,' or have I been a fool, convincing myself of something I merely wanted to believe?" I couldn't stop such questions from coming.

The fact was, there were many girls Joby would have to let go of for us to have a chance. Once again, completely out of character for me, I decided to press forward. It was a bit like throwing caution to the wind, but I couldn't get over the feeling that something bigger than me was leading.

I never pushed Joby. But I confess that the challenge I'd embraced wasn't easy. In the moments that I felt undervalued, unloved, or jealous, I made a conscious effort to choose love. I also made myself irresistible, making it difficult for him to pass up spending time with me in order to spend time with anyone else. I don't mean that I changed myself for Joby. Rather, I worked to be my best self, which was something I'm pretty sure none of those other women were attempting to do in their own lives. It set me apart. In the end, the other girls never had a chance.

Two years after our meeting Joby and I were engaged in Isla Mujeres, Mexico. On a scuba dive trip through the huge fresh water caverns of the Cenote, decorated with stalactites and stalagmites, Joby pulled out a clamshell with a ring in it and, in this underwater palace, asked me to marry him. Six months later, at a beach ceremony in the Bahamas, we were wed.

It was crazy how fast things unfolded. How did I feel so connected to someone I had just met? Why did I feel so compelled to go against conventional wisdom in order to develop a relationship with that person? What had driven me to stick in there with someone who, in certain ways, looked like he might be serious trouble? I know now that there was a reason that other relationships in both Joby's life and my own had failed to flourish. Every rejection, every fear, every parting was directing us to something better—to a shared destiny. Every 'no' had moved us closer to the right 'yes.'

Looking back, in fact, I can see God's divine hand leading me throughout my life. I see how previous relationships prepared me not just for a lifelong relationship with Joby but also, and even more importantly, for my ultimate relationship to God himself. He used all of those moments, relationships, and circumstances to draw me near.

Everyone has experienced something that changed them in a way that made it impossible to go back to the person they once were. Throughout life I have always had a plan for myself; an image of what my life would be. But God had a greater plan for me than I could have ever planned for myself. When God brought Joby into my life, I somehow knew He had sent him to me for a purpose. Joby's entrance into my life was, without a doubt, my turning point. My healing has come—continues to come, in fact—primarily through the challenges he and I face together. The lessons I have learned with him are the very reason this book exists. He was worth the wait.

As a mutual teacher and learner on this journey, Joby will attest he has learned a number of lessons of his own. The greatest of these, he tells me, is that of reading closely the people and the environmental cues he once over looked. He is honing in on his intuition daily. He has also learned to trust. He recognizes that, unlike his previous relationships where people frequently used each other to advance their own interests, I always have *his* best interests at heart. Perhaps most importantly, Joby has learned a great deal from me about patience. He and I are each unique individuals, often with very different preferences. We've made a commitment to be together for the rest of our lives, which doesn't always come easily for the best of us, never mind someone who once solved many problems by simply walking away. Today, he has instead increasingly adopted my practice of breathing before responding.

Together, we've learned important lessons of forgiveness and humility—being able to acknowledge when were are wrong. We do not go to bed angry. Instead, we focus on the love between us and the love given to us from God. We've also had to grow in our patience.

Joby and I never tire of our journey together. Rather, we know that time is short. That reality shifts our perspective in a way that allows us to live as if each day could be our last together. After all these years, Joby and I not only love each other, we still really *like* each other. Not only have we learned from each other, through our relationship we have come to lean on God even more. We are thoroughly invested in and enjoying the great adventure God has set before us. It's not something we write ourselves. It's something to which we have aligned and to which we know we are called.

Reflect for a moment. Is there a person in your life right now who is helping you to grow in a healthy way? That person may or may not be a romantic partner. It might be a parent or a friend. In my case, many of my greatest lessons have come by Joby, who is now my husband. He has been the most consistent conduit for me to learn what love means, allowing me glimpses into the bigger picture of what it means and how it feels to experience God's love—what it is to lean on Him. And here is the key: As much as I love Joby, I love God more. That single truth is actually mind-blowing, because God loves you and me even more than we could ever hope to love him. His love is—almost—unfathomable.

The powerful attraction Joby and I felt towards each other was undeniable. Though I did question myself for a brief second, I quickly came to my senses. It sounds cliché, perhaps, but we were like two magnets being pulled together. It's one of the ways God works to allow us to get an inkling of that *almost* unfathomable love He offers. He draws people into our lives so that we have the opportunity to learn the lessons we need to grow. Those people, whoever they happen to be, challenge us to live outside of our comfort zone. They draw us closer to our Creator.

> "And now these three remain: faith, hope and love.
> But the greatest of these is love".

> — 1 Corinthians 13:13 New International Version (NIV)

That's a message straight from God to us.

We already know you have faith; you are reading this book. If you are willing to do the work to implement these principles, we know you also have hope. And the greatest is love—which we are all learning everyday.

The Apostle Paul tells us that even if we have faith that could move mountains, without love we are nothing. In fact, without love there is no hope. In John 15:12, Jesus exhorts us to "love each other as I have loved you." God's immense love for us surpasses the heavens and earth. He loves us without end. But how can we, in our earthly state, ever hope to measure up to that kind of boundless love? Is it even possible to love others as God has loved us? And how do we even answer that question until we determine what love is?

Love can mean plenty of different things to different people. While it may not be complete, I've adopted what I consider to be a good working definition: to voluntarily do what is best for another person. Sometimes, that means saying no to our own or another's desires and sometimes it means saying yes. It is about leveraging the information we have, along with our sense of what God is telling us, in order to take the best course of action possible in the situation in which we find ourselves. It won't always be easy; it will however be worth it.

Let's go back to an earlier example to shed light on this concept. Make believe for a moment that a person in your life is tightly clinging to the victim mindset. After a long period of time, they haven't been able to shake it. You have done everything you could possibly think of to help remedy the situation. At this point, love may require that you bless that person and walk away for a time. That course is likely not just what is in your own best interest but also theirs. You can let them know you will be there for them should they need you, but for the health and healing of you both, it's necessary to remove yourself from the situation temporarily.

I realize that saying no can be difficult, but there's good news. Putting someone else's best interests first in a *healthy* way automatically puts you and the relationship in a stronger position—one that is more likely to yield success.

This thing we call life gives us many learning opportunities, and learning to love is one of the biggest lessons of all. To best love ourselves and those with whom we share this life, we must actively choose love at every potential cross road. As we choose healthy commitments to each other, we foster conditions that have the highest likelihood of yielding the greatest good. If the story you've been telling yourself lacks love, free yourself from it and replace it with a new story of unconditional love for yourself and others. As we face our fears of inadequacy, faith will emerge that love actually abounds.

One of the chief problems I've encountered in my own life in striving to achieve such faith concerns a reality of human psychology. The human mind uses opposition to make sense of reality. Examples include love versus hate and safety versus danger. Living in love enables us to release condemnation. Remember, condemnation is actually rooted in fear. While often tempting, it makes us feel superior only by focusing on making another *wrong* or *bad*. It therefore separates us from others instead of building valuable bridges.

Love, on the other hand, feeds our own spirit and feeds the spirits of others. When we reject fear and embrace love, we ground ourselves with inner peace. Doing so helps us to ease misalignments in our relationships and create a powerful ripple effect that has the potential to restore harmony in much wider circles. Again, when we focus on our own healing and allow others the grace to do the same, it empowers both our light and theirs to shine brighter.

Is it possible to choose love in every circumstance?

We can certainly try. Our blueprint—what we are at our core—springs from a foundation of love. God loved us from the moment He created us. In fact, He created us precisely because He wanted a loving relationship with us. This truth makes love a possible and right choice in all situations. The question is only whether that is the choice we will make.

At this point, in the history of the world, only Jesus has lived a perfect life. Happily, God does not expect perfection from us. From the moment He created us, He knew there would be times that we would stumble or downright fail. It's okay. We have the ability to lean on God, to cast our fears and worries on Him—to rely on his power rather than our own. Though it might seem contradictory, when we do lean on God, we actually gain strength through Him. With God, love is the undercurrent that is ready to surge to the surface of every situation, to heal and free us. While we're going to make mistakes, in every circumstance that we choose love, we allow it to dominate our reality. Love is the answer, no matter the question.

The BREATH Of Life

And the Lord God formed man of the dust of the
ground, and breathed into his nostrils the breath
of life; and man became a living being.

— Genesis 2:6-7 New King James Version (NKJV)

The sweet sound of a ukulele dances in my ears as if the notes are bouncing off the sheet music and into my head. As the man on the beach strums, I am whisked away to a place of peace and calm.

When I arrive in Hawaii, the first thing I like to do is to go straight to the beach. I get out of the car and run to where the sand meets the water. I feel the warm sand squishing between my toes and hitting the back of my calves as I race towards the healing ocean. I breathe in the heavy, salty air. I feel the light breeze tickling my skin, reawakening my physical being and recharging my whole self. The sun shines down, wrapping its rays around me welcoming me back from elsewhere—particularly the "mad-land," the local term for the mainland, so termed because many locals believe you'd have to be mad to live anywhere but Hawaii.

When I reach the water's edge, the frothy salt water swirls at my feet, and I feel all my tension dissipate. I am in heaven. My heart overflowing with joy. I stretch my arms open wide and begin to spin, wrapping myself in the perfection of the moment. The islands are an extraordinary, happy vortex that suck you in, pouring love all over you like a spigot that cannot be turned off.

ALOHA

If I were pressed to give a worldly location that feels most like home, then Hawaii would be it. There are many amazing places around the world, but Hawaii holds a special place in my heart. When I am on my way, I want to dance with excitement that I'm returning. While there, I experience healing. When I leave, it calls me back. Quite simply, Hawaii breathes life into my soul. If you've ever visited Hawaii, you likely know exactly what I mean. For these reasons, wherever I travel, I take the spirit of the islands with me: *aloha*.

More than a simple greeting, aloha actually describes and imparts a state of being, presence, and love. In fact, at its root, aloha has deep meaning. *Alo* signifies "the presence of," while *ha* is "breath." Native Hawaiians once greeted each other by placing their noses together and sharing a breath, much as God did when He breathed into our nostrils the breath of life. When settlers came to Hawaii, they were termed *haole*, or without breath, because they did not greet the natives by sharing the essence of life—breath.

For these reasons I bring the spirit of Hawaii with me everywhere I go. I greet others with the term aloha instead of the standard hi or hello. This personal tradition not only helps me feel connected to the islands when I'm away, it helps me to live in the world and relate to others in the way that I wish.

An active and powerful place, some say the healing people experience while on island stems from the energy the islands transmit and their ability to align the systems of our bodies. There may actually be a scientific foundation for aspects of this claim. Our bodies generate electromagnetic fields. That's not mumbo-jumbo. It's fact established by at least two decades of scientific research. Of our various organs, it's now known that the heart generates the human body's single largest electromagnetic field. That field is detectable by others and can be recorded on medical devices. Interestingly, this discovery lends a certain credence to the Eastern spiritual notion of *chakra*, rooted in the belief that each of seven major points of our bodies— the heart being the most important—emit a subtle energy.

In recent years, scientists have worked to perfect ways not only to measure the fields our bodies create—particularly those of the heart and the brain—but also to see them. The HeartMath Institutes website, for example, states: "The electrical field as measured in an electrocardiogram (ECG) is about 60 times greater in amplitude than the brain waves recorded in an electroencephalogram (EEG). The magnetic component of the heart's field, which is around 100 times stronger than that produced by the brain, is not impeded by tissues and can be measured several feet away from the body with Superconducting Quantum Interference Device (SQUID)-based magnetometers."[5] Others have begun to discuss the fact that mood can impact our personal electromagnetic field.

In the book *Science Of The Heart*, the HeartMath Institute provides an in-depth analysis of the study of the energetic communication of the electromagnetic field of the heart.[6] Data from studies outlined in the book strongly suggest that magnetic signals radiated by the heart of one individual are capable of influencing the brain rhythms of another. I don't claim to understand how this process works. However, I do find it fascinating that we can register the electromagnetic signals and information patterns emitted by another person.

HeartMath's research also suggests that the electromagnetic field a heart generates can be perceived consciously. We spoke about intuition earlier in the book. Is it perhaps possible that what we conceive as intuition could, at least in part, be attributed to our subconscious response to the electromagnetic fields of others? Is it perhaps possible that such information, invisible to the naked eye, allows us to detect and understand key information about people in an instant?

These same veins of research also point to the distinct possibility that we have the capacity to affect others in close proximity to us through the electromagnetic signals the heart generates. If this possibility turns out to be true—and it seems likely—then fostering and self-regulating positive emotions would be not just mentally and spiritually valuable but also physically beneficial. It would mean that we actually have the ability to re-pattern our electromagnetic baseline.

Let's look at just one important example of how the electromagnetic fields that hearts generate likely impact one another: the bond

---

[5]   https://www.heartmath.org/articles-of-the-heart/science-of-the-heart/the-energetic-heart-is-unfolding/

[6] Rollin McCraty, *Science of the Heart, Volume 2: Exploring the Role of the Heart in Human Performance* (Boulder Creek, CA: HeartMath Institute, 2015).

between a mother and child. How is it that a mother always seems to have an innate sense about her baby? Could it be that part of her keen awareness is an ability to sense subtle signals and changes in the the electromagnetic energy of her child, or even differences between her electromagnetic field and that of her baby? If so, that's miraculous. God's design is always perfectly crafted.

In considering the potential implications of the electromagnetic nature of the heart, God's careful exhortation in Proverbs 4:23 seems more than profound:

> Above all else, guard your heart, for everything you
> do flows from it.

> — New International Version (NIV)

God has known since the beginning of time what science is only fairly recently discovering: Our hearts are relational. We live heart-centered lives.

God Breathes Life Into Us

Mauna Kea rises impressively from the Big Island of Hawaii. The tallest volcano in the world when measured from the sea floor, its summit was considered by ancient Hawaiians to be the realm of the gods. Spiritually speaking, many people today still give great significance to the connection point between heaven and earth. Such places call up for us the moment when God breathed life into us, taking us from dust to cherished beings made in His image.

It's amazing just how powerful breath can be. I attended my first breath workshop while in Hawaii. It was life-changing—not least in the way I began to notice and think about the nature and significance of breath and its interdependent relationship with the heart.

When each of us is born, there is a moment of anticipation in which our parents, the doctor, and everyone else in the delivery room holds their breath, waiting for the baby to cry out. Crying signals breath. If the baby does not take its first breath, there is no life. At the end of our lives, it is said that we take our last breath. When we stop breathing, our connection to life on this plane ceases.

In fact, the book of Genesis tells us that God created Adam from the dust of the earth, then breathed life into him. It's a dramatic and compelling concept. The vocabulary term used to express it—*ruah*—is no less so. In ancient Hebrew, *ruah* does triple-duty, signifying wind, breath, *and* spirit.

It's far from accidental that the concepts of breath and spirit, in particular, became fundamentally and inextricably linked. We were always meant to understand that God breathes life into and through us. The fact that *ruah* is used 389 times throughout the Old Testament provides an additional sense of the importance assigned to this conflation of meaning. It is also found in the ancient Greek of the New Testament, where it is expressed as *pneuma*.

Just as the Bible describes God breathing life into us, it similarly describes breath as going out of us when we die. Once God releases our breath—our spirit—we return to the dust from which we started.

The breath of God that lives within us is vital, then; one might say, vitality itself. Breath reminds us of who we are and where we came from. It is innately tied to the divine purpose God gave to each of us—what we are meant to accomplish in the short time each of us has been granted here. As if to underscore this truth, the book of Psalms refers to one's life as "but a breath." Human life, we are reminded, is limited and transitory. It is also precious, not to be wasted.

Despite these strong spiritual implications, breathing is something we usually do without conscious thought. In fact, most of us tend to take breathing for granted. But don't all of these linguistic clues suggest that we're meant to pay much closer attention?

It turns out that being mindful of our breath can relax our body, bring focus to our mind, de-escalate an emotionally charged state, and reduce our level of stress. Changing our breathing exercises a strong impact on our circumstances and well-being and fosters self-healing.

It's worth looking at some examples of how breath and breathing change in order to start considering our respiration more consciously.

It's easy to notice a shift in our own respiration when we're stressed out in heavy traffic, for example. Our breath becomes shallower with anxiety or heavier with frustration. A shallow breath is passive in nature, air is brought into the upper portion of our chest and lungs but doesn't reach the lower portion of our lungs down to our diaphragm. Shallow breathing causes us to take more breaths per minute than the deep relaxed breathing that fills our lungs. The heavy breaths of frustration are active. In exasperation we push the breath from our lungs as if sighing. Neither of these forms of breathing are particularly helpful. First, they do not supply our body with the adequate amounts of oxygen we need. Second, they exacerbate the emotional state in which we already find ourselves.

When you're on an island, you're on island time. The clock and the pace of life slow. Breathing often changes to match the rolling of the waves, becoming more balanced and deeply rooted.

The calming of our breath begins by taking elongated breaths of air in through the nose until the stomach expands. This outward manifestation of the diaphragm and stomach muscles at work is how we know our breath is fully reaching the depths of our lungs. A corresponding exhalation involves expressing air slowly until your diaphragm contracts.

We take about 26,000 breaths each day. Caught up in our day-to-day life, there are frequently times when we're on the brink of losing it. We get frustrated or angry, and our breathing alters. Similarly, our breath increases when we are scared. It's a natural physical response. As we seek to satisfy the heart, the healing power of our breath and the life it literally breathes into every situation becomes an imperative consideration. Becoming aware of our breath, in fact, is a practice ignored all too often in recognizing our current state, what is truly important, and what we may need to let go of.

There's a simple breathing exercise that I use in order to achieve exactly those ends. It's a tool that can be used anywhere. I'm sharing it here, so you can do just that. Whenever you feel stressed, anxious, overwhelmed, or just need to clear some space in your head, this valuable exercise will help you to transform your outlook.

1. In a comfortable position, close your eyes and relax your body, releasing the tension in your muscles.
2. Draw a breath in through your mouth, then exhale, pushing the air out through your mouth.
3. On your next breath, breathe in through your mouth and out through your nose.
4. Next, breathe in through your nose and out through your nose.
5. Finally, breathe in through your nose and out through your mouth.

This represents one cycle of the breathing exercise. You can continue this same cycle of breathing until whatever was plaguing you fades in intensity. Typically, three cycles will make a tremendous difference in perspective.

Change Begins Within

If you want to awaken all of humanity, then awaken all of yourself.
If you want to eliminate the suffering in the world, then
eliminate all that is dark and negative in yourself.
Truly, the greatest gift you have to give is that
of your own self-transformation.

— Lao Tzu

There are two different ways to go about living life. We can live life
for ourselves, nourishing our worldly desires; or we can choose not
to conform to the ways of the world and live the life God has called
us to. As spiritual beings, we are called to live in the world and yet
to resist conforming to it.

As human beings we are innately compelled to build the world in
which we live. Growing closer to God and living as He guides and
outlines makes it possible to do so. God instills life and purpose
within us so that we can make his love visible to the world through
his word. The question is, where will we place our focus? Will it be
on the things we want to nurture in the world—or something else?

The second chapter of Ephesians tells us that we are God's
workmanship, "created in Christ Jesus for good works, which God
prepared beforehand, that we should walk in them." (verse 10,
English Standard Version) We are each a single, crucial piece of a

multi-billion piece puzzle; without us and the specific contributions we were created to make, the puzzle can never be complete. The good works that have been set out for us to do make each of us essential. Right now we may only see our one piece, not the whole picture. That's okay. Sure, we can focus on all the terrifying, negative stories that dominate the world around us, the stories that inundate the news stations blaring from our televisions. However, if we constantly focus our awareness on the negativity in the world, rather than the ways in which we can make a difference, we are only contributing to the problem.

What if we each made a shift to awareness? What if we could remain aware of what is going on around us without allowing it to consume us? We can't go through life ignoring the constructive or destructive things occurring. We can, however, choose to tune out manipulative negativity that is regularly being pushed on us. We can instead realign with love and the higher mission for which we've been sent.

A war is constantly being waged for our consciousness. Society tends to condition us to false desires, and distorted behavior patterns. Consumerism and addiction are just two of many examples. Moreover, the media, politicians, and others regularly thrust negativity and fear upon us, dividing us into opposing categories— the "haves" versus the "have nots," men versus women, white versus people of color, and on and on it goes. The insanity of constantly battling others and separating ourselves from perceived enemies ultimately sinks us. Yet, when we connect back to God, truth always surfaces, helping us to find solutions to the problems we face rather than perpetuating them.

Rather than getting caught up in life, then, aren't we better off getting caught up in the *purpose* of life?

If we want a good and positive future, we have to *look* at the good and the positive. I'm not saying don't be realistic. I'm not talking about magic formulas. Rather, I'm saying that reality can, in large measure, be something we build through the choices we make.

Nowhere does this truth become more clear than in relationship to the company we keep. God tells us in Proverbs 22:24-25, "Do not associate with a man given to anger; or go with a hot-tempered man, or you will learn his ways and find a snare for yourself." (NIV) The principle is difficult to refute. If we associate with those wrongly focused, we hinder our ability to build anything positive. Such people bring never-ending conflict into our lives, because their emotions and modes of communication corrupt the good that God is working to cultivate in us. Unless we avoid such people, we run the risk of taking on soul-destroying attitudes and behaviors.

The fact of the matter is, though, that we're frequently going to encounter people who won't take us in a good direction. Sometimes they will be people we've just met. Sometimes they're people we've known for a long time but are simply no longer healthy for us. Happily, when we remain open to God's leading, not only do we get quicker at discerning who is healthy for us and who isn't, we also grow more adept at handling the unproductive negative emotions that others want us to take on. Remember, we need to focus on our own lessons and permit others the freedom to learn those meant for them. We ensure this proper order by observing the situation and lovingly refusing to absorb what belongs to someone else. With a little practice, releasing emotions that belong to others can become as simple as saying, "This is not mine. I release it." Letting go and allowing God to do the work in both the situations and people we encounter feeds our ability to live in gratitude in whatever circumstances arise; it's how we can begin to fully accept God's will as our own.

Only by allowing God to change the ways in which we respond to the people and life situations we encounter—can we respond optimally to the call on our life and change the world in the ways we're meant to do. There is no way around the risk such a choice entails. God's ways are usually not our own. But God's ways are also always infinitely more perfect than our own. That particular truth raises some some questions, because if God's ways are different than our own, following God involves two risks: first, letting go of what we know; second, letting go of what we expect. Neither is ever easy.

What do you want to see happen in your life and in the world? Are you willing to relinquish fear, trusting and leaning on God to do more amazing things in and through you than would otherwise be possible? Are you ready to take action and come fully alive? Will you embrace the lessons that God has already brought you through and stay open to those that have yet to unfold? Are you ready to experience a wealth of blessings that only reliance on God can deliver?

The work we do here is our own heart made visible in the world. That's why it's so important to keep an *open* heart. It's built into each of us to desire positive connection to others, and through others we come to know ourselves better. What happens, though, if we block the message we were sent here to convey—if we withhold the talents and skills we were meant to employ and share? What are the untold losses if we shortchange ourselves and others of the purpose for which each of us was made? In *It's a Wonderful Life*, director Frank Capra explored this question in an iconic manner that has been appreciated by millions of people since its 1946 release. The film's central character, George Bailey, discovers with the help of the angel Clarence that even when our presence and contributions seem insignificant to us, the people around us and the world in general would be far poorer without them.

Isn't it time, knowing this truth, to shine your light in the world—to reject the false messages you've absorbed about yourself? Indeed, isn't it time to live truly believing that you are an integral part of God's grand design and that the world actually needs what He has uniquely given *you* to offer?

Have you ever heard someone say, "There is nothing I can do about it," or, "It's out of my control?" These are excuses. The truth is that there is so much each of us can do in our personal lives to impact the world in positive ways. Nourishing our spirit with the right food ensures that we can speak love into the world through our words and actions. Speaking love into the world, in turn, ensures that we won't make just some tiny or temporary dent while we're here but rather an impact of eternal significance. In fact, when we choose to ground ourselves in the power and conviction of the word of God—when we remember that we are His creations, designed to do remarkable things in the world—we have access to a source of internal power that is greater and infinitely more permanent than the world itself.

Trust God to change one heart, and it can change everything. Will you let Him start with yours?

The end of one journey is the beginning of another.

Let's continue the journey together
at: <u>WeeksAbroad.com</u>

About the Author

Stephanie Weeks is a social entrepreneur and wellness advocate. A thought leader, she writes for various food and travel outlets. You can follow her adventures at <u>WeeksAbroad.com</u>

The cover for Food Of The Spirit is the beautiful creation of my friend Robin Emmerich. Her brand, Beauty & The Mess, empowers women to walk unafraid into a little chaos, stand out in a crowd, and face life's challenges head-on. Robin's work encourages interaction with art in a new way, out of a desire to bring more love and beauty into the life of the viewer. I deeply appreciate her mission and its synergy with the message of Food Of The Spirit.